WHOLE-PET
HEALING

A Heart-to-Heart Guide
to Connecting with
and Caring for Your
Animal Companion

Dr Dennis W. Thomas

HAY HOUSE

Carlsbad, California • New York City • London • Sydney
Johannesburg • Vancouver • Hong Kong • New Delhi

First published and distributed in the United Kingdom by:
Hay House UK Ltd, Astley House, 33 Notting Hill Gate, London W11 3JQ
Tel: +44 (0)20 3675 2450; Fax: +44 (0)20 3675 2451; www.hayhouse.co.uk

Published and distributed in the United States of America by:
Hay House Inc., PO Box 5100, Carlsbad, CA 92018-5100
Tel: (1) 760 431 7695 or (800) 654 5126
Fax: (1) 760 431 6948 or (800) 650 5115; www.hayhouse.com

Published and distributed in Australia by:
Hay House Australia Ltd, 18/36 Ralph St, Alexandria NSW 2015
Tel: (61) 2 9669 4299; Fax: (61) 2 9669 4144; www.hayhouse.com.au

Published and distributed in the Republic of South Africa by:
Hay House SA (Pty) Ltd, PO Box 990, Witkoppen 2068
info@hayhouse.co.za; www.hayhouse.co.za

Published and distributed in India by:
Hay House Publishers India, Muskaan Complex, Plot No.3, B-2,
Vasant Kunj, New Delhi 110 070
Tel: (91) 11 4176 1620; Fax: (91) 11 4176 1630; www.hayhouse.co.in

Distributed in Canada by:
Raincoast Books, 2440 Viking Way, Richmond, B.C. V6V 1N2
Tel: (1) 604 448 7100; Fax: (1) 604 270 7161; www.raincoast.com

A catalogue record for this book is available from the British Library.

ISBN: 978-1-4019-4764-4

This book is dedicated to all the caretakers and their pets who have allowed me to be a part of their lives throughout my career—including Clarence and Carol Haught, Karen Owen, Marjorie Duncan, Sue Edwards, LaVon Stuart, Barbara Campbell, Jim and Jean Yaudes, Hugh and Tekla Bear, Russ and Bonnie Haleen, Barb Christofferson, Tina Gates, Rick and Marsha Dial, Denise Morris and Mary Beth Healey, Sydney Watson, and hundreds more who have brought me to the realization that people have the ability to return the unconditional love that is given to them by their pets. They have been the inspiration for and the meaning of my career. Also, to Kathy, Tian, Bethany, Nicole, Jen, and all the many staff members whom I have had the good fortune to work with, who have dedicated their lives to assisting pets in their healing, using compassion, patience, and devotion far beyond my capabilities.

CONTENTS

*"But souls that of his own good life partake,
He loves as his own self; dear as his eye
That are to Him: He'll never them forsake:
When they shall die, then God himself shall die:
They live, they live in blest eternity."*

— HENRY MORE (1614–1687)

INTRODUCTION

Removing the Blinders

The last thing a veterinarian wants to do is start off the day by euthanizing a pet. For a person whose career is intent on promoting healing and prolonging life, there is something paradoxical about having to reverse that state of mind. It is certainly our obligation to relieve pain, and euthanasia is the ultimate treatment for that; however, I can safely say there is not a veterinarian anywhere who doesn't wish he or she could erase that part of the job description.

I thought it was going to be that sort of day of having to put a pet to sleep—but it was far from it. It was a day that would instead remind me to remove the blinders of expectations and move forward in the awareness that all things are possible.

I opened the door to the small room that was used for euthanizing patients. It was designed for comfort. It had a small exam table, two cushioned chairs, soft lighting, and pleasant pictures on the wall that did not display pets playing with their caretakers. I didn't know the middle-aged man and woman with a small, orange Manx kitten that looked to be about four months old. I had never examined the kitten, but the couple—Fred and Dora—had told my receptionist that he needed to be euthanized.

Before I could introduce myself, Fred's eyes welled with tears and he asked in a desperate voice, "Doc, can't you do anything?"

"Why don't you start by telling me what is going on?" I said.

Fred composed himself and continued. "Alex—that's his name. He wasn't even our kitten. He was our neighbor's kitten, and we would see him outside in our yard at times. Sometimes we would share our cat's treats with him. We never even noticed that there was a problem."

He explained that one day the neighbor, whom they admitted they hardly knew, came to their door and told them he and his family were moving. He said that they couldn't take the kitten with them and were going to have to find him another home. The neighbor wondered if Fred and Dora might like to have Alex.

After a short discussion, the couple agreed that it wouldn't be a problem, since the kitten lived outside and seemed comfortable in their backyard. It did not take Fred and Dora long, once they started paying attention to little Alex, to realize that something was wrong. The kitten seemed to drag his rear legs behind him, and it became obvious that he could not control his bowel and urine functions.

After a thorough investigation on the Internet, the couple came to the conclusion that the kitten had a congenital disease called Manx syndrome. Manx cats have no tails because they carry a defective gene that doesn't allow proper development of the tail. Unfortunately, sometimes the defect is more extensive, and the result is an improperly developed spinal cord, above the tail. This underdevelopment often leads to the inability to walk, urinate, or defecate normally. There is no traditional Western treatment for this disease, and euthanizing the animal is usually recommended to eliminate its suffering.

After an extensive neurologic examination, I agreed with Fred and Dora that their tentative diagnosis was correct, and that it was true that euthanasia was the standard protocol and was probably in the kitten's best interest.

Obviously not content with my recommendations, Fred pleaded, "But isn't there anything you can do besides euthanasia?"

It was at that moment that I was really hit with the pain and frustration of admitting I had nothing to offer except a way to "relieve the suffering."

The tears were flowing from Fred's eyes now, and the emotions in the room were palpable. In a desperate attempt to offer some hope, I blurted out, "Well, maybe we could try acupuncture."

Holy smoke! Did I just say that? I felt like Ralphie in the movie *A Christmas Story* when he spouted profanity in front of his father and immediately knew he was in big trouble. I was keenly aware that I, like Ralphie, might be in a position to metaphorically "get my mouth washed out with soap."

I took a deep breath and explained that I was in the process of learning veterinary acupuncture and Traditional Chinese Medicine (TCM), and that I had a network of more experienced professionals I could reach out to for advice. "If you're willing to let me try, I'd like to explore this option."

"Yes!" Fred said emphatically. "Anything, if it might give him a chance to live." A hopeful smile now crossed his face. His eyes locked with mine, and I knew I had given him something to hang on to. Dora's expression did not change. I was quite sure that if my treatment failed, she'd be the one with the soap in hand.

That evening I contacted a group of veterinary acupuncturists and asked if anyone had any experience treating kittens with under-developed spinal cords. I felt sure that I would get some positive input. The next day when I checked my messages, though, all I heard were crickets. No responses to my request. Finally one well-respected veterinary acupuncturist called several days later and left a message: "I seem to remember treating one of those kittens several years ago, but don't recall the outcome. Good luck, and let us know how it goes."

Great, I thought. It had become painfully obvious that I was alone in this ordeal. I picked up the phone and called Fred and Dora.

"Unfortunately, no one has responded to my request for information," I explained. "I have no guidelines, so if we start with the acupuncture treatments, I will be doing this without any experience and not much guidance. But I'm still willing to try if both of you are. I suggest that we treat him with acupuncture once a week for four weeks and see if we get any response."

Fred and Dora agreed with my plan, and we scheduled the first appointment for the next afternoon. Alex seemed willing to accept the treatment as I began placing needles in acupuncture points to move energy along the spine. In subsequent appointments, I added electrical stimulation to the needles that were placed along his back.

Electrical stimulation acts to enhance the effects of regular acupuncture and can be a very beneficial adjunct to certain acupuncture points.

After four weeks, we started to see improvement in Alex's nerve function, and he was walking with more control. At the sixth week, the kitten could control his urine and bowel functions, and at the eighth week, Alex was happy and playful, with a normally functioning nervous system.

Needless to say, Fred and Dora were filled with gratitude as they witnessed Alex's transformation into a healthy, normal kitten—and I experienced a profound shift in my approach to veterinary medicine.

PART I

CONNECTING WITH YOUR PET HOLISTICALLY

CHAPTER ONE

THE SHIFT TOWARD HOLISM

"True fortitude of understanding consists in not letting what we know to be embarrassed by what we don't know."

— RALPH WALDO EMERSON

I've been a veterinarian for more than 30 years now. Throughout most of this time, I, like many vets, focused on a traditional approach to medicine and surgery. I was your typical go-getter, always pushing to try to figure out the thorniest problem. But about a decade ago, I got tired of hitting dead ends. I got tired of telling people to choose between Option A and Option B, especially when neither option was favorable.

I started finding myself drawn more and more to stories from clients who told me things like, "You know, a sister of mine out in California had a dog with uncontrolled seizures, so she went and had acupuncture done on the dog, and now he's doing really well." My imagination was captivated by the possibilities.

Besides an intense, natural curiosity, what's always driven me in my work is an awareness of the incredible connection that exists between people and their pets, including me and my own. *What* is

3

going on there? I wondered. *How can we do more to help these creatures who so graciously share their lives and their wisdom with us?* I just knew it was time to go further than I had ever been before, and so, after nearly two decades of traditional veterinary practice, I went back to school to learn Chinese medicine . . . and all the pieces of the puzzle started fitting together.

Making Miracles the Norm

In my practice, I continue to incorporate traditional approaches, but alongside such complementary modalities as Chinese herbalism, acupuncture, Reiki, and even visualization and meditation. I've built a reputation for healing animals that other veterinarians have written off—but it's not because I have some magic power. The truth is that little "miracles" like Alex happen all the time.

As I've shifted the focus of my practice toward promoting healing rather than simply fighting disease, it's become increasingly important to me to help my patients move in a direction where we consider these "miracles" the norm. Through this book, I hope to help *you* move in that direction as well.

But how do we get to that place?

The answer is simple: by opening our minds and expanding our approach. In doing so, we can shift our beliefs to encompass the possibilities other modalities of healing offer. This doesn't mean we "throw out the baby with the bathwater" and forsake our traditional medical system. Instead, we gratefully accept the methodologies we were raised with, acknowledging the many benefits they have brought us. Yet we also become aware of the limitations of this system and open ourselves up to alternative or complementary healing methods. Then, as these new methods prove effective, our beliefs become knowledge, and we share our experiences with others and create new opportunities for *them* as well.

The problem, though, is that the vast majority of people who seek complementary health care for their pets are not getting their information from veterinarians, but instead from friends, neighbors, magazines, and so on. The reason is that most veterinarians today are uncomfortable providing information about nontraditional methods, which are deemed untested and unproven.

In my previous practice, I did a lot of work with paralyzed dogs— I'm talking about pets whose caretakers told me their other veterinarians did an MRI and swore their dogs would never walk again. Well, 18 out of 19 of those dogs *walked* out the clinic's doors. It was then that I decided to form a practice of my own devoted to holistic pet care. One of my fellow veterinarians saw this demonstration of the efficacy of complementary medicine with his own eyes, yet to this day he has never attempted to use it on a patient. The paradigm he's stuck in— that most veterinarians are stuck in—makes it very difficult to attempt (and for many, to even see) what lies beyond its boundaries.

My experiences have taught me that pet caretakers are desperate for somebody who can give them guidance and instructions, or at least who can point them in a direction that offers more options than just A or B. It is my hope that reading this book will help you find a veterinarian you can trust to do exactly that, and that you will have enough reliable information at your disposal to get you started in exploring holistic pet care—without resorting to or relying on hearsay.

What Is Holism?

Throughout the United States, an enormous movement has been building toward a more "natural" form of health care. One of the most significant expressions of this movement is the concept of "holism" or "holistic medicine." (The word *holism* is derived from the Greek word *holos,* meaning "whole.") Holism is the belief that any system can be best understood when it is viewed as a whole instead of as the sum of its parts. But this is not the way we humans have understood ourselves for most of our existence.

Since the advent of modern medicine, the approach to health has been in learning the science of the body, in the hopes that, with this knowledge, doctors will be able to comprehend how disease occurs and what needs to be done to cure it. The more closely something is looked at and examined, the more clearly it can be understood. At least, this is science's historical perspective: In order for the body to be understood, it needs to be broken down into pieces; then those pieces need to be broken down into smaller pieces, and the focus becomes narrower and narrower.

Today, the physical body is seen by most scientists as a conglomeration of cells working under the influence of biochemical reactions. Disease is understood to be the result of disruption of those mechanisms by known or unknown causes. The problem with this perspective is that, in our attempt to better learn the body's functions, our awareness has been led away. We've disconnected from a larger truth: that the material body is a mere microcosm existing in a larger macrocosm where all things are connected.

We know, with the discovery of the subatomic world, that even though something appears to have a solid form, such as a rock or a table, if broken down to its smallest components, it is nothing but tightly packed bundles of energy. Well, this may seem to still be in line with the scientific approach that looks at smaller and smaller components of the body in order to comprehend how it all works together. But here's the problem: Our bodies—and our pets' bodies—*appear* to be distinct, but are in fact, at the tiniest observable realm of existence, *not very well defined at all.* From the perspective of the energetic nature of all matter, we can expand our understanding of the body and its energetic connection to things that surround and influence it.

To put it another way, like a single drop of water in the ocean, our material bodies are distinct, yet part of a greater being; and in order to see the whole picture, we must open our awareness to encompass a greater truth. This is *holism.*

Holism and Awareness

Humans have a great capacity to perceive events from different perspectives. Take this scenario, for example:

Imagine that you're walking along in a beautiful forest, surrounded by unspoiled nature. You feel the sun on your face. You hear the birds singing and the wind rustling in the trees. The forest is a gathering of trees that reach to the sky. Without knowing, you have become one with your surroundings. There is no need to think about things or *do* anything. You just allow yourself to be present in the moment, in a consciousness of acceptance and gratitude.

Suddenly, you look down at the pathway and—*oh, no!*—there's a rattlesnake moving toward you. Immediately, instinctively, you move into fight-or-flight mode, and you turn around and run away. Without your conscious direction, your body reacts: Your adrenal glands release cortisol, increasing your heart rate and providing a burst of energy to allow you to escape. *Whew!* In no time, you're back to a safe area, and you begin to relax, knowing that you're okay.

What you have just imagined is the wonderful ability for the mind and body to accommodate situations in the blink of an eye. In a matter of seconds, you have gone from a state of consciousness that was expanded, consisting of soft borders and a feeling of oneness, to a contracted state of consciousness focused on survival.

Almost all of us have this ability. Unfortunately, most of us don't take the time or know how to *become aware* of our state of consciousness during our daily lives. Without awareness of how we're focused, we allow ourselves to remain trapped in that survival mode, our consciousness driven by external forces. We're like the ricocheting balls in an arcade game, reacting moment to moment, maintaining fearful, often negative states of consciousness. And we also see ourselves as very, very isolated—from one another, from nature, and from everything around us.

If you're reading this book, you've probably sensed that there's more to your existence than this narrow band of reality. Maybe you've experienced other states of consciousness, as in our nature-walk example, which allowed you to connect with something greater than yourself (or even simply with another being). When we become aware of our ability to move from an expanded state of consciousness to a narrow one when needed *and back again,* and we condition ourselves to live our lives with this awareness flexibility, then we are experiencing holism: the awareness and acceptance of all states of being, all states of consciousness. Among many other benefits, we regain control over ourselves. Life is no longer a pinball game, or perpetual fight-or-flight mode. We are no longer isolated entities whose inner conditions are dependent on a closed system of cause and effect. We live in a world of endless possibility.

A Holistic Approach to Pet Care

As I said, in our busy, day-to-day lives, we often get stuck in a reactive state of consciousness. This is also characterized by a narrowed perspective of our thoughts and emotions, in which we forget or never even realize that we have other means of direction and guidance. In time, we become so dependent on our thoughts and emotions that we suppress the subtle movements of life nudging us toward larger truths. Eventually, we lose touch with those subtle, heart-centered feelings that point us inward instead of outward.

When we regain the awareness of our innate guiding systems and use this awareness in developing our relationship with our pets, we come to realize the immense joy they can bring to us, the guidance they offer, and the opportunities they provide to reveal the larger truths about ourselves. We also come to recognize a new approach to caring for these loving animal companions as our connection deepens and our awareness of their needs—and our options for meeting these needs—broadens.

As we maintain a holistic perspective regarding our pets, we stay open to the awareness of the interconnectedness of all things, understanding that we cannot discount any part or piece and its influence on the whole. We find that the emotional energy in our home environment is just as important for our cat's health as the type of food we give her, and that our *intention* to heal our ill dog is just as powerful as the pills and procedures we administer to him. The holistic perspective of ourselves and our pets keeps us aware that there is always something larger than our present reality and keeps us moving forward in our understanding.

As we begin our journey together, I'm going to ask that you remain open to possibility. In the early chapters of this book, we'll take a step back from pet health care in particular to explore the scientific underpinnings of holistic health care in general.

Wait—did I just say that holism was scientific? Yes, I did! And you're about to find out why. So, relax and allow your awareness to expand, to let in some new ways of looking at the world and understanding your relationship to your pet.

Once we get through the science, I'll guide you more specifically in caring for your pet, including how to find a veterinarian who supports your holistic perspective and offering a new way to nurture your pet's body, mind, and spirit from the time you come into each other's lives to the time when you must necessarily say good-bye.

Before we begin, let me congratulate you on taking the first step of picking up this book and being willing to explore your options for caring for and connecting with your beloved animal companion. In this book, you're going to learn that pet health care encompasses a whole lot more than vaccinating your pets or treating them when they get sick. It's more than just feeding your cat the best foods or ensuring your dog gets enough exercise.

Each one of us who has pets can feel that there's something deeper in that relationship than what we can explain. No longer should we have to look through a straw and believe that what we see is the whole world. Through my experiences, I know not only that something amazing is happening just *beyond* the focus of our consciousness, but that there's something there beneficial both to our pets and to us, if only we allow ourselves to experience it. So let's begin doing that, right now.

CHAPTER TWO

BEYOND MODERN MEDICINE

"The cure of the part should not be attempted without the cure of the whole."

— PLATO

Scientific methodology has helped the medical profession eliminate many horrible diseases and continues to benefit our quality of life. However, our health-care system is entirely based on the scientific belief that the body functions purely chemically, and chemicals are required to aid its function or to restore normal function following disease. Therefore, our system narrows our treatment options for fighting disease to primarily chemical compounds known as pharmaceuticals or drugs.

It is widely known here in the United States that the pharmaceutical industry has become a powerful entity and has enormous control over the direction of health care. This goes for people and animals alike. Most of the medical research is funded by a handful of huge pharmaceutical corporations with the intention of finding new drugs that will help fight disease. This is certainly not a bad intention, but it is also bound by the limitation of its focus. On the other hand, studies dealing with methods of healing not involving drugs are poorly funded and therefore few and far between. This has slowed the tide of shifting perspectives regarding holistic treatment options, though the tide is nevertheless rising steadily.

Today, in the West, it has become increasingly popular to seek out a more natural, holistic approach to life. Nowhere is this more apparent than in our approach to health and well-being. However, thanks to pop culture and general misinformation, many people who are drawn to holism either don't know what to expect or are unnecessarily timid. When it comes to holistic medicine, what you bring to the experience significantly impacts what you get out of it.

Your intentions, your emotions—everything about you—can influence your pet's healing process on an energetic level. One of the reasons I talk a lot about energy and quantum physics in my practice, and in this book, is that it allows me to extend a bridge between what many people perceive as "voodoo" and the "real medicine" they've been exposed to by the established Western scientific tradition. But we'll come back to that in some detail later. First, let's get a good foundational understanding of what holism really is, so that we can better understand the challenges associated with its acceptance in Western culture.

The Philosophy of Holism

Holism in medicine, whether for you or your pet, goes far beyond the introduction of complementary methods of treatment. Certainly, the methods extend our options, offer alternatives to treatment with fewer potential side effects, and reduce the overall cost for health care, but the real benefits come in accepting the philosophy of holism. We realize we are affected not only by those things that we know and understand but also by forces that we can't and may never be able to explain.

Try to get a scientist to prove the existence of love. He will probably tell you that, from a scientific perspective, this emotion does not exist because he cannot prove that it does using the methods and practices accepted by the scientific community. No, at best, love can only be inferred to exist by how it is expressed.

However, if we can change our perspective and accept that love is *a subtle energetic force,* then we can witness this emotion moving life in miraculous ways, without ever understanding how it does so. We don't need a scientific analysis to prove to us that love exists. We believe that it does; therefore, it is expressed in our experience, which acts to reconfirm our belief. We might choose to exhibit a loving feeling toward another, and in return we might receive a loving feeling directed toward us. We are moved emotionally in a way that we identify as a loving feeling, and it defines the emotion *love.* We now have experienced love without needing proof of its existence. If you can be okay with that, then you will probably be okay with holism. (At least, more okay than your average scientist!)

Quantum Physics' Contribution

Leaving love aside, the health industry—from the universities, research laboratories, on down to doctors' offices—clings to the methodologies science uses to define the material universe as the *only* way to approach health and disease. If it can't be proven in the laboratory, then it can't work. Period. When the rules governing matter can't explain the paradoxes that arise with regard to the body's functions, then doctors turn their heads the other way and say, "That doesn't count."

This sort of reaction reminds me of the movie *The Life and Times of Judge Roy Bean,* where Judge Bean, played by Paul Newman, is presented with a law book that contradicts his logical ruling. After careful study of the finding in the law book, Judge Bean rips the pages from the book, therefore eliminating the discrepancy.

So what kinds of paradoxes are we talking about? A good example lies in the ability of parts of the body to receive information and direction from other parts for coordinated movement. Imagine a ballet dancer doing a beautiful pirouette on a stage. The scientist can explain to us that the display is driven by physiology: The body has an autonomic nervous system that can control itself without the conscious mind directly involved. In other words, the mind doesn't have to think, *Left leg bend, right leg straight, muscles of flexion contract, muscles of extension relax,* and so on in order for the pirouette to happen. However, even the body's autonomic nervous system has to send signals from the brain to the effector sites (muscles, blood vessels, lungs, heart, and so forth) for every movement that is occurring while this wonderful artist is performing. In just a few seconds of her performance, her body has completed thousands of functions.

In the laboratory, neurophysiologists have determined that the speed of the nerve impulses responsible for these actions and functions is far too slow for all this to be possible. Well, then how can you explain the dance? Don't ask. They won't tell you, because they can't. They can't explain it in the laboratory; therefore, it can't happen. Ouch.

And yet, the body's nervous system *can* perform at these speeds (obviously), and it *can* in fact be explained—not by biochemistry, but by quantum physics. So much of how quantum physics (the science of subatomic particles) works is still a mystery, but explorations on the frontiers of science have revealed a number of fascinating energetic principles. For example, *quantum entanglement* is a phenomenon that occurs when pairs or groups of particles interact in such a way that you can't just look at the behavior of one component—you must look at the quantum state of the whole relationship. Experiments have proven that particles separated by large distances somehow "know" what is happening with each other and react accordingly. Moreover, they do so instantaneously, faster than the speed of light . . . which is supposedly impossible. Einstein aptly referred to entanglement as "spooky action at a distance."

Another example that we'll look at more closely in a moment is the Heisenberg uncertainty principle. This one's a bit complicated and mathematical, but the gist is that the more closely we look at one aspect of a particle, the less sure we can be of its other qualities. It's been proven that human observers actually impact the outcome of measurements at the quantum level, which is why so many resources have gone into creating expensive laboratory environments with machines, like particle accelerators, that take humans out of the equation.

And yet, though many forms of complementary medicine are based on these and other proven energetic principles, such modalities are still difficult for the medical community to grasp. To understand the true nature of our reality, we need to expand our approach, not narrow it. This doesn't simply mean that a doctor now includes the importance of diet and physical surroundings in his analysis, although these factors should be of concern. Indeed, to be truly holistic, we must look at *the subatomic environment* and *the effects of energy on the body*. This requires an understanding of the physical dimension, of course, but also—and perhaps more important—how the material body relates to the nonphysical or energetic dimensions: in other words, those layers of reality we can't easily observe.

We're going to delve deeper into the "how" behind holistic health care and energy in the next chapter. For now, start to open your mind to the idea that, while our understanding of the world has throughout history been limited by our culture, science, and technology, that understanding is constantly expanding as advancements are made and as a function of time. We may *never* be able to scientifically prove how any system works (including the body) in its entirety—or we may figure it all out in an astounding breakthrough a year from now. Regardless, we must be okay with not having the full picture without shutting ourselves down to the results we *can* access. Only then will we allow ourselves to move beyond our comfort zone into a new way of thinking.

Modern Medicine: A Fear-Based Approach

Many years ago, when I was in veterinary school, we were taught about the importance of the triangular bond between pet, caretaker, and veterinarian. The bond represents several perspectives, but for me none was more important than the bond of trust between caretaker and veterinarian—after all, my patients and their caretakers count on me as a veterinarian for my knowledge and experience, and they look to me for guidance in their times of need. What could be more important than earning this trust?

The sad truth is that this essential bond is increasingly threatened and strained. These days, most veterinary colleges are teaching their students to practice from a "defensive" approach. Students are told that any client who brings in a pet has the potential to sue them if a mistake is made. The net effect is a generation of new veterinarians who have that little voice in the back of their head whispering, *Don't do anything that might get you sued.*

This fearful approach to medicine leads to an exaggeration of the narrow-minded Western perspective built on the foundation of a "nothing but the facts" policy. Why would veterinarians dare offer alternative modalities of treatment to a client without having irrefutable proof they work? The answer is that most will not.

Most fear-influenced clinicians find safety in dealing with the laws of probability. For example, say that a pet has been diagnosed with a terminal cancer. The veterinarian reviews options for treatment and presents them to the caretaker. He explains that if this treatment is used, statistics show that 30 percent of the time, life expectancy is increased by as much as one year. Statistics also show that without the treatment, the life expectancy drops to six months. Now science wants to look a little deeper and introduces the probability factor, which is like a safety net for the facts. It issues a probability factor of 0.05, which means 95 percent of the time, if the treatment is used, the results will be as predicted. This is the scientific methodology's attempt at ruling out the unexpected. Western-trained clinicians are comfortable with these results, as they feel safe in presenting this data to the caretaker. It essentially rules out any surprises.

The problem with the fear-based approach to Western medicine is, because it is predictable, it sets both parties up to have certain expectations and beliefs. If a veterinarian suggests surgery for a pet to remove a cancerous leg and gives the caretaker documentation that shows the low probability of something occurring that is not routine, and then that unexpected thing happens, the veterinarian will most likely be held accountable. Now not only is the veterinarian scrambling to defend himself, but the client is also scrambling for an answer as to why something unexpected happened. Unfortunately, neither party had their expectations met; as a result, the intent of helping the pet became secondary.

My experience with a patient named Lucy illustrates this point very well. The young Labrador retriever had developed severe seizures that might occur as often as six times a day. The grand-mal episodes would leave her incapacitated, and her quality of life was extremely poor. After a thorough workup by Lucy's regular veterinarian, her caretaker, Ann, was referred to a neurology specialist at the local veterinary college. Over the next week, Lucy was given every test available, ranging from blood screens to brain scans. The diagnosis was epilepsy, and as a matter of course, she was placed on a combination of antiseizure medications.

When I saw Lucy the first time, she could barely stand up due to the side effects of the drugs. Her eyes were glazed, and she responded slowly to all stimulation. She no longer wanted to play or interact with the family. Ann explained she had been informed that, in all probability, this was what she could expect for Lucy's quality of life. Essentially, Lucy's caretaker was told that scientific research and statistics suggested a high likelihood that the dog would never improve. So, a choice was presented to Ann: allow Lucy to live like this or put her to sleep. From this perspective, we have eliminated all uncertainty and can provide an evidence-based probability. We know what to expect if we do or do not take certain actions.

Fortunately for Lucy, Ann wasn't sold on the story these other clinicians provided. We performed acupuncture on Lucy, and I prescribed her a therapy involving Chinese herbs and diet changes. Within six months she was off all medications and was seizure-free. She lived a normal, happy life with her family for another 13 years. I can only imagine Ann's emotions during the conversation she had with those who tried to convince her to give up on her beloved dog and accept their very negative version of what Lucy's life was destined to be like.

I have asked veterinarians over the years why they don't refer more patients for complementary treatments if they have no other viable options. The answer has consistently been: "If I send someone off for treatments that are not proven, and they don't work, then I will be blamed."

This is a classic example of clinicians' fear of accountability overriding the possibility that their patients might benefit from the treatment. What they fail to realize is that, because of the fear, they have placed themselves in a no-win situation. If a veterinarian fails to recommend complementary treatment for the pet and the caretaker finds out later, then the veterinarian will be forced to explain why that option wasn't presented.

I once treated a paralyzed dog that had been worked on by her regular veterinarian, a colleague whom I knew well. After months of unsuccessful Western treatment, the caretakers were told all options had been exhausted, and the vet recommended that the pet be euthanized. Fortunately, a neighbor encouraged them to explore alternatives, and the caretakers took it upon themselves to find another way. After we treated the dog with complementary therapies—and he was walking again—the caretakers were furious that their veterinarian had not suggested any other routes, and they were grateful that I had.

The Scientific Method

One of the biggest challenges for proponents of holistic health care is that the philosophy of holism stands in contrast to the scientific method, our current process for evaluating and understanding systems. As I've mentioned, the scientific method functions by breaking down the system, part by part, in order to explain how it works. Someone comes up with a theory and creates an experiment to prove that the theory is correct, and then other people repeat it to see if they get the same results. If enough people do, everyone starts to say, "Okay, it's not theory anymore; it's fact, it's law."

There are two problematic parts here: (1) The more concrete we make something out to be, the more we think we understand it; and (2) we trust only what can be explained when broken down into components that are measurable and testable in a laboratory setting (in other words, that which follows the material laws of science). This approach, in its fundamental attempt to narrow its focus, naturally lends itself to a self-limiting outcome.

Analyzing a system such as the body and how it functions from a scientific perspective, a "just the facts" perspective, requires rationality and reasoning. These mental processes are considered functions of the brain's left hemisphere. The perspective of holism originates in the brain's right hemisphere, considered the home of intuitive and creative functions, both of which are required for a holistic perspective to take root. The thing is, the more that people rely heavily on logical reasoning, the more they limit their capacity for intuitive, empathic perceptions. When the left hemisphere is active for extended periods of time, the right-hemisphere function is suppressed. In time, all perspectives are coming solely from a narrow scope. This is why I say that the scientific method is self-limiting with respect to medicine. Holism doesn't discount the scientific method. It just says that the scientific method is looking at the world through a straw.

Conventional medicine essentially ignores anecdotal evidence because such results cannot be duplicated in the laboratory with a double-blind study. But complementary healing modalities are moving beyond this limitation. For example, if I place an acupuncture needle into an acupuncture point on the inner wrist of a dog, the acid produced in the stomach will be reduced by about 10 percent. This protocol and the results can be reproduced time and again and are documented and predictable, but the mechanism of *how* this works cannot be proven by scientific analysis. For the scientific method, remember, it isn't enough that something is repeatable. It must also be possible to break it down into its components and explain how it works using the laws of material science.

Ask the healer how this acupuncture treatment works, and she will tell you it has to do with *Qi* (pronounced "chee"), which is energy moving throughout the body. But the scientist says, "What is Qi? Show it to me." And, so far, we aren't able to do so. Though we can repeat the results of acupuncture, we cannot explain *in material terms* how or why these results occur. Something is happening that we can't "see," much less measure. Therefore, medical and veterinary clinicians alike refuse to accept this treatment protocol. And, perhaps more important, they are afraid to be held accountable for results they can't bring themselves to feel confident in expecting. Most clinicians perceive Qi to be some sort of mystical explanation that fails to stand up to the standards of science. What they do not understand is that what the Chinese refer to as *Qi,* the quantum scientists now refer to as *subatomic or subtle energy.*

Placebo, Nocebo, and Caretaker Expectations

One sunny afternoon while I was a senior veterinary student, we soon-to-be-graduated veterinarians were summoned to the large animal facility for a presentation. We sat quietly on the bleachers as several of our clinical instructors moved around the room. Suddenly, the door opened and in walked a clinician leading a horse.

This was a horse we all knew. He was a retired racehorse with a history of severe arthritis and intense pain, and he had been brought to our large animal clinic. Over the previous few months, our veterinary clinicians and students spent countless hours administering to this poor horse. His pain was so severe that if you placed your hand on his back, he would try to collapse to his knees. Despite all our modern methods of treatment and many forms of medications for pain and inflammation, he continued to suffer.

After a few minutes had passed, the door to the room opened again, and a small contingent of Asian veterinarians were led in. We were told that they were from Japan and were touring the United States and visiting our veterinary colleges. One of the Japanese veterinarians began examining the pained horse. He gently moved his hands along the animal in a precise manner and made comments to his colleagues as he worked. After a few minutes, he began to place acupuncture needles in strategic locations across the horse's body. Some of the students began to giggle and make comments about the "voodoo medicine."

The needles were left in the horse for about 20 minutes, then removed. The veterinarian walked over, took a saddle blanket and saddle, and placed them on the animal. He then mounted the horse and rode him around the room. It was obvious that the horse was pain-free! The room was silent, and the students and clinicians alike sat in disbelief. You could quite literally hear a pin drop; it was that quiet.

🐈

Although acupuncture and Traditional Chinese Medicine were introduced to the United States over a century ago, these methods of treatment are primarily ignored by the medical community—both human and veterinary. The reason is because breaking the body down into its various components and looking at the complex array of biochemical actions and reactions does not reveal the secret of either of these healing modalities. At best, medical professionals have attributed observed results to the *placebo effect.*

The placebo effect is the unexplained phenomenon wherein a patient is given a pill that has no medical benefit whatsoever and is told that it will make him or her better. About 33 percent of the time, the patient will improve based solely on the belief that the medication will allow him or her to do so. Recent research indicates that the placebo effect might be even greater, up to 90 percent. Some medical practitioners view these results as a kind of a joke, a trick that our minds play on us, rather than something to be applied positively—or, better still, as evidence that there's more going on at the energetic level of mind-body connection than the scientific method can measure.

One day I was having lunch with a friend at a local restaurant and was explaining how much the use of acupuncture had benefited my patients. Suddenly, a man sitting at a nearby table interrupted me. "How dare you make those claims," he said. "I am a doctor, and you know as well as I do that the benefits of acupuncture are based on nothing more than placebo."

I turned and looked at the physician, knowing that he truly believed that acupuncture had no benefits beyond tricking the mind. I said, "How can you explain my results as placebo when all my patients are animals? I'm a veterinarian." With a stunned look on his face, he turned away and finished his lunch.

Not all physicians share this doctor's negative opinion of placebos. A 2012 *Time* special edition, *Alternative Medicine,* reported that a U.S. survey of internists and rheumatologists found that about 50 percent of those surveyed admitted to regularly prescribing placebos. If patients strongly believe that a medication will cure them, then it often will, and there are doctors who are willing to use this tool to help their patients even if they don't fully understand how it works.

From where I'm sitting, what the placebo effect confirms is that the mind has the ability to control the functions of the body. If we *believe* that we will heal, then we most likely will. Whether the treatment consists of pharmaceutical administration or surgery, the mind ultimately holds "trump" over the body in influencing healing. In the *Time* special edition, author David Bjerklie states in his article "The Magic of the Placebo" that "when a placebo works, it doesn't mean a patient's symptoms . . . aren't real. It just means that the neurochemical changes produced by the expectation of relief are just as real."

A related phenomenon, less frequently mentioned, is the *nocebo effect,* the shadow manifestation of placebo. Nocebo occurs when the patient believes that the treatment will have little or no effect. For example, if the patient is told that there is no successful treatment for a disease, then the patient's mind will direct the body in a way that does not allow for healing. If a doctor tells her patient that a treatment will have serious side effects and that life expectancy will be shortened, then you can bet that there *will* be side effects and that the stopwatch has been set for ultimate death.

It's clear that placebo and nocebo affect our own health, but how do they affect our pets' health? Animals don't tend to concern themselves with wondering whether or not a treatment will work, so it can't just be some kind of Jedi mind trick, as I pointed out to the doctor who overheard my lunch conversation. I'll discuss the energetic connection between us and our beloved pets in detail in a later chapter, but basically, what we *believe* about a treatment will have a significant effect on the actual outcome for our pet. The energetic connection between pet and caretaker overcomes the physical boundaries, and the energy of our beliefs is a major factor directing or inhibiting healing.

As I stated earlier, in order for the medical profession to open itself to the possibilities of complementary treatments, it must soften its demand for the "proof" it has historically been most confident with. By simply opening to these potentials, the mind moves into greater balance, uniting its logical, rational tendencies with its intuitive, empathic capacity. This will be true for individual professionals as well as the "group mind" of the medical community. And with this balance, characteristics such as empathy, nurturing, and compassion will become a more regular part of the health-care process. These factors are critical for effective healing.

The Uncertainty Factor

Chuck Yeager, the first pilot to break the sound barrier, is attributed with saying, "Just before you break through the barrier, the cockpit shakes the most." Well, the world of health care is surely shaking now. Will we make it through to the other side or retreat back to what's comfortable, despite its limitations?

Case in point: There is an acupuncture point located on the human foot that, when stimulated, can effectively change the position of an unborn child just before birth. Research indicates that when this point is activated in mothers whose babies are in the breech position (a situation most hospitals resolve through Cesarean-section delivery), the baby repositions itself into the normal presentation and the birth process proceeds naturally *greater than nine times out of ten.* Despite the awareness of this procedure, most obstetricians refuse to attempt acupuncture because they cannot explain to the mother how it works. Instead, the trend for surgery continues. In a documentary I saw on this subject a few years ago, one young mother who had been successfully treated with acupuncture in this manner commented, "I don't really care how it works. I was supposed to have surgery before the treatment, and after the treatment I had a normal delivery and no surgery was needed. That is all that matters."

The fear of accountability has unfortunately continued to escalate the defensive mind-set of the Western clinician, unnecessarily limiting the options for all of us. Today I see that accountability has trumped trust between clinician and caretaker—the basis of the all-important triune bond I alluded to earlier—but if blame is to be cast, it should be upon both parties. Both must be willing to look at options without clinging to predictable outcomes, especially if these outcomes are poor at best. For us to have hope that we can move into a more holistic approach to health care, we need an open mind that can handle the "uncertainty" factor. And we must remember what really matters: our pets' well-being.

Reestablishing Trust

Unfortunately, the fear-based approach to clinical health in human and veterinary medicine is moving more and more in the direction of limitations and predictability. Medical technology has been a great instrument in helping this along. In the exam rooms of both physicians and veterinarians, the norm is becoming a hands-off approach to diagnosis. Instead, the clinician stays within the realm of predictability, with the use of ancillary testing to make a diagnosis, and research and statistics to give a prognosis and determine treatment options. No one wants to leave without clear expectations.

The alternative is reestablishing trust between caretaker and clinician. The clinician has to believe that decisions can be made without fear of liability if things don't go as hoped, and the caretaker has to trust that the clinician's intention is to help the patient above all else. Once the trust has been established and the fear is removed from the process, then both parties can look at all options and select one based on the best interest of the patient, without limiting their choices to unfavorable options simply because they are predictable and probable.

To approach medicine, veterinary and human alike, in a more holistic manner, we have to move beyond our fearful tendencies. We have to be willing to step outside our comfort zone and believe that if our intentions are good (aimed at establishing normal health), then we can accept the outcome no matter what. If we can muster up our faith in the face of uncertainty, then we, too, can experience the miracles we hear about.

Once we witness these events that defy scientific explanation, we can become teachers and spread the word to our friends and colleagues. In time, the standards will change, and the medical community will have to face a decision: whether to stick to its stringent philosophies or embrace a new, expanded perspective that will take us all beyond the limitations of the scientific method.

CHAPTER THREE

UNDERSTANDING THE ENERGETIC BODY

*"All matter originates and exists only by virtue of a force. . . .
We must assume behind this force the existence of a conscious
and intelligent mind. This mind is the matrix of all matter."*

— ATTRIBUTED TO MAX PLANCK,
NOBEL PRIZE–WINNER IN PHYSICS

I always hated physics. It wasn't hard to understand, but I never could get over feeling that I just didn't like it. This was a little difficult for me emotionally as a young man, because I was led to believe that boys should like this branch of science. After all, physics classes came with little toys: pulleys, transformers, and so on. Those were acceptable forms of entertainment, and most of my male friends did love to play with the toys, but I suspect it wasn't the science that drove their enjoyment.

It didn't help that in my high-school physics class, while attempting to straighten out the parallel wires of the electric transformer my best friend plugged in, I was blown out of my chair. Nor did it help that my unsympathetic teacher, instead of showing me compassion and concern, used me as a teaching example of what it is like to have electric current running through a blob of organic mass. Yes, just what every teenager wants—to be called a blob! Then, as if that wasn't enough to turn me off to physics, the most difficult professor I had in my college career, of course, taught that class. The only two things that I left with were the first and only C I ever received in college and his bizarre theory that the effects of the porcelain toilet on the anatomy would lead to the downfall of humanity.

Little did I know that my abhorrence of the physical science of matter and its principles would allow me to easily move into the study of energy and quantum physics. In the previous chapter, I introduced the basic concept of the energetic body and how it relates to quantum physics. Now, in this chapter, we'll dive more deeply into the subject.

You might be thinking, *Why do I need to read so much about quantum physics and energy in a book about holistic pet health?* Good question. Remember, quantum physics is about energy, and everything—*everything*—is composed of energy: this book, the chair you sit on, your computer, rocks, plants, your thoughts and emotions, your body . . . and your pet's body. No exceptions to the rule—all things are energy.

If we can learn how energy affects us and how we use it to live our lives, then this knowledge can help us direct our lives in a way that will most benefit us. That includes directing our health and the health of our pets.

Quantum Physics: The Energetic Key

Let's go back in time, look at history a bit, and see which events led us to our current understanding of the world.

In ancient times, healers were simply those people in the tribe who had some spiritual awareness, often known as "medicine men" (and medicine women) or shamans. For the most part, people were okay with healing being mystical—they didn't really know how anything worked. In the blink of an eye, historically speaking, a transformation then occurred. Organized religion (in the West, the Catholic Church) began to convince people that their dogmas could explain the facts of the universe, especially regarding what happens to the body before, during, and after life on Earth. Most people accepted this without question, but many a wise person was belittled or persecuted for taking a stand against the medieval church and its beliefs.

In one such heroic instance, a fellow named Nicolaus Copernicus (1473–1543) was bold enough to voice his opinion that the earth was not the center of the universe. Instead, he proposed a *heliocentric* model—that the earth revolved around the sun. Although this view was contrary to the church's belief, it opened the minds of future intellectuals and eventually led to confirmation that this theory was indeed correct. But, more important, this was a decisive event that instigated the Scientific Revolution, in which humankind's need for control started driving us to figure everything out and create a logic that would explain our experiences. This is where we started looking deeper and deeper into the material world for answers.

Another meaningful turning point in history hinged on the discoveries and theories of Sir Isaac Newton (1643–1727). From the time the apple fell and hit this chap on his cranium, science has used his laws of motion and universal gravitation to explain everything from the orbits of planets to how the body works. This is the same physics that I revolted against in school and the same principles that govern most high-school science classes to this day.

My bias aside, Newtonian physics is a wonderful contribution to science, but being enamored of its principles is starting to get old. Newtonian theories explaining our reality have been accepted by the scientific community for so long that any attempt to explain reality from a different perspective is understandably rejected. Up until fairly recently, scientists were at a point where they actually started to believe they might know all that they could possibly know about the laws of the universe.

The famous quote "Just when you thought you had all the answers, they changed the questions" seems appropriate here. In the early 20th century, a few physicists started thinking outside the box and played with some new mathematical formulas. For instance, Max Planck's $E = hv$ explained the energy of waves, and this enumeration was followed by Albert Einstein's theory that a wave could be described as a particle, and vice versa. This combined effort led to a unified theory from which we derive the concept of wave-particle duality. And did this ever take the lid off Pandora's box!

The discovery of quantum physics set off a chain of events that pitted the materialists (Newtonian-science team) against the energetic, nonmaterial physicists (quantum-physics team). You are probably once again thinking, *What does this have to do with my pet's health?* Hang on a bit, and you'll see.

Newtonian physics deals with the laws of material objects. Well, that makes sense until you break down the material object to reveal its subatomic nature (energy). Once matter is broken down into its energetic components, the components change their character and no longer play by the rules governing material objects. The new rules they follow are the theories of quantum mechanics.

Today, *most* branches of science have accepted quantum physics, with much anticipation of what lies ahead as new technology is giving laboratory proof of what was once just a mathematical formula on some chalkboard. There is, however, one exception to this great forward movement. Can you guess what it is?

The medical establishment has drawn a line in the sand regarding acknowledging the laws of quantum physics. The *why* is up for debate. Some say it is a safety precaution (remember what I said about modern medicine's fear-based approach?), while others say it is monetary. No matter the reason, the health-care industry continues to hold tightly to the belief that Newtonian principles are the only possible means of understanding how the body functions.

Energy and Health

With antecedents in the 1800s, quantum physics really began to shift scientific thinking in the early 1900s with the principles discovered by the aforementioned Max Planck and Albert Einstein. Einstein's work, in particular, led to the acceptance of the dual nature of things at the subatomic level, meaning that the tiniest components of matter exist as both a wave and a particle at the same time.

This wave-particle duality flies in the face of the traditional scientific method. Quantum physics incorporates unpredictable outcomes—quantum physicists refer to this as the *uncertainty principle*—and science cannot deal with the unpredictable. It would have to redefine itself. Science views the unpredictable as fearful instead of unlimited.

Imagine the physical body being reduced to its organ systems—then further reduced to tissues, cells, molecules, and atoms. This is pretty much where scientists have stopped with regard to medicine and health. They have attempted to explain form and function from this perspective. Unfortunately, despite their reductionist tendencies, they refuse to continue to reduce the body's components beyond this point. This is where quantum physics does its thing.

When the atoms are broken down into their subatomic parts, the new laws of quantum physics have to be applied. The atom's smallest fundamental units, *quanta,* are tiny packets of pure energy. Things really start to get interesting when physicists begin to explore the functions of these quanta. It seems that their nature is determined by the observer's preconceived notion or perception. In other words, *they actually change properties according to what the observer believes them to be.* That's right: Our very thoughts have an observable, measurable impact on the energy that serves as the subatomic foundation for all matter in this world.

Another significant revelation of quantum physicists concerns the makeup of the body. Traditionally, scientists have believed that the body, when broken down to its smallest components, consists of groups of atoms (particles) separated by large spaces or voids. These voids supposedly account for the majority of the subatomic or energetic body. But quantum physicists have proven that the voids are energy as well, and that the energy in the void also makes up the atoms. Therefore, energetically speaking, there is no true separation between atoms.

The significance of this finding is that the energy and information to control the functions of the atoms—which, in turn, make up individual cells, which make up the tissues and organ systems, which ultimately make up the body—can easily be transmitted at speeds that explain the capability of the ballet dancer to execute her pirouettes, as discussed in Chapter Two. But if quantum scientists can account for how the multiple components of the body can work together at warp speeds, how can they explain who or what is directing the action?

Einstein said that science would bring us back to the ultimate truth of the mystic. In a way, he predicted that science would come full circle from Copernicus, who initiated centuries of efforts to get away from not-knowing, to the mystic who says, "There is something out there in control of us—that controls *everything*—and I can work with that, even if I don't know precisely what it is."

Let's look at another example of that possibility. Most of us have seen a large flock of birds flying in complete synchronization. Hundreds move across the sky in perfect harmony in a wavelike pattern akin to a cosmic dance. There is no chaos or conflict, no individual birds crashing into one another. Scientists can only theorize how this happens, but thus far their theories have failed to hold up under scrutiny. Frankly, they don't really know how it works! What is directing the birds to fly in this manner, and how do they accomplish it without chaos? Scientists can't tell us.

Now imagine the physical body acting in the same manner. All the energetic components are dancing to the harmonic rhythm of perfect synchronization. In fact, the body's components, from the subatomic level on up, *have* this ability to dance in the same coordinated perfection as the flock of birds—without conscious direction. According to scientists, the nervous system (the brain, spinal cord, and peripheral nerves) is responsible for this behavior. But the scientists themselves have proven that the nervous system is far too slow and unorganized to coordinate this perfect dance of energy. Many quantum scientists thus believe that the information and direction comes from an energetic field outside the body.

Have you ever tried to rhythmically beat a drum? You will soon realize that the more you think about creating a rhythm, the less you are able to do so. However, if you stop thinking about it, the rhythm starts to flow naturally.

Imagine that there is a universal energetic field of infinite intelligence that directs the birds to fly in harmony—and directs the rhythms of the entire universe. Stretch your imagination to believe that this same energetic field runs through your whole body, your pet's body, and everything in your world. If you can imagine this rhythmic energy that creates form and function, then you can understand how the body works its miraculous capabilities. You will also begin to understand what *really* directs healing.

The Body as Energy Fields

Consider the physical body (yours or your pet's) as a large bundle of swirling waves of energy. Let's imagine that it is yellow. Now imagine that there are other bundles of energy within the yellow energetic bundle. There is a blue bundle that represents your heart energy, an orange bundle that represents your liver energy, a purple bundle that represents your kidney energy . . . and one for each of your organs and tissues, including your blood and lymphatic system.

Now imagine energy bundles for each individual cell of the body. Go further and imagine that there is an energetic bundle for each cellular component, all the way down to the DNA and its chemical components. This mental illustration is a representation of what some quantum scientists refer to as *body fields, morphogenic energy fields,* or the *energetic body*—the foundation for energy medicine, mind-body healing, and intuitive or distant healing. These energetic fields have also been invoked to explain how the body's cells communicate with one another and as a source of information and direction (though we have yet to *prove* if these fields are the origin).

Einstein is quoted as saying, "The field is the sole governing agency of the particle." What makes the existence of energy fields important with regard to body function and health? The answer lies in the mechanism for transmission of information throughout the body. Cells cannot function without information to instruct them. From the time the first cell divides and creates a physical body—throughout the cell's many regenerations, disruptions in health and healing processes, and ultimate demise—it has been directed by some process that up until now has never been identified.

With the discovery of the cell's genetic components (DNA, RNA, and chromosomes), fascinated scientists have been focused on the likelihood that genes were solely responsible for the cell's functions. The hypothesis became so widely accepted that, in time, it was viewed as scientific fact—that is, until the Human Genome Project concluded a few years ago. Until then, scientists spent their time probing the genetic characteristics in an effort to identify the code that provided the answers explaining the body's development and functions. Expectations were high that genetics would explain not only how the cells function but also how genetic imperfections led to disease, with the hope that cures for those diseases would be just around the corner.

One thing was certain going into the project, they thought: Genes are responsible for protein production, and the individual cellular protein's activity is responsible for the cell function. But they needed to find that absolute connection between genetic makeup and cellular function to get the ball rolling.

In the end, there were many surprises. First, geneticists determined that there are about 25,000 genes in the human genome. However, there are hundreds of thousands of different proteins in the body. If we do the math, it becomes obvious that there cannot be one gene responsible for each protein unit. This meant that one gene must obviously have the ability to produce more than one protein unit. The biggie came with the discovery that the gene itself is not responsible for its own activity—*something outside the gene is controlling the genetic performance*—and, with that fact, the gene lost its standing as the king of the hill. Science could no longer assign sole responsibility for the function and characteristics of an individual to the genetic makeup—or blame it for the failure of its system. Oops.

If the genetic makeup is not responsible for initiating the function of the cells of the body, then what is? According to Bruce Lipton, Ph.D., in his book *The Biology of Belief: Unleashing the Power of Consciousness, Matter & Miracles,* cellular information originates in the external environment. In his lab, Dr. Lipton purposely removed the nucleus, which includes all genetic material, from a cell to determine the effects on its function. He found that although the genetic material was absent, the cell continued to function normally. Eventually, individual cell protein units died due to their natural aging process, and without the genetic function of the cell to manufacture the protein, the cell, too, died. But the genetic material proved only to serve a purpose in protein production, not in initiating cellular function. Something in the cell's environment did that job instead.

What does it mean that the environment controls the cellular activity? It means that factors such as nutrition, toxins, emotions, and thoughts all play a role in how the individual body cells are going to perform. Environment trumps genetics.

Dr. Lipton, in his appearance in the documentary *The Living Matrix,* refers to research on families who have a genetic predisposition to forming cancer and have adopted children *without* those genetic predispositions; in time, the rate of cancer formation was the same. According to Dr. Lipton, the potential for cancer in those studied was determined by the environmental dynamics in the family, factors such as perceptions, beliefs, diet, and so on. This also explains why many individuals in families with the genetic makeup to predispose them to diseases such as diabetes never develop those diseases, while others do.

The old belief *Heart disease runs in my family, so I probably will develop it as well* is not necessarily so. We can no longer blame the genetics. This is an extremely empowering bit of information. It frees us from the *belief* that something is going to happen, and that is one of the major factors in *preventing* it from happening.

Scientific research has proven that emotional disturbances, such as stress, have deleterious effects on the physical body. The sustained release of cortisol due to emotional or physical stress causes harmful effects, including reduced immune capabilities, increased blood pressure, and predisposition to cancer formation. But the scientists have had a hard time identifying just *how* this happens.

Dr. Lipton determined that the energy associated with negative emotions and thoughts triggers certain cellular functions via the receptors located on the surface of and within the cell's membrane. The energetic profile, or wave characteristic, of those emotions stimulate the cell to improvise and perform in ways other than its normal function even though the cellular genetic makeup should be instructing it to do otherwise. Again, environment trumps genetics.

So to summarize, the physical body has a certain finite number of genes, responsible for protein production, which in turn is responsible for cellular function and performance. A source other than the genes *initiates* the activity of the cell, although the genes play a role in that performance.

To make things perfectly clear, imagine the genetic makeup of the body as a piano with all the white and black keys arranged in a specific order. Each cell has the same makeup of white and black keys. Even though it has the potential to play every melody that has ever existed, the cell will only perform according to the pianist who controls the key selection. One moment the pianist might be playing Bach, and then Beethoven the next moment. As I mentioned, the genetic components of cells "perform" by receiving information primarily from an energetic source *outside* the cell.

Let's look at an example of environmental effects on the body's health. Most people know that if the body is exposed to radiation at high levels or for prolonged periods, there is the potential for the development of cancer. The radiation from the environment triggers the cell-membrane receptors to alter the function of the cellular protein, and the cell changes its genetic expression and no longer functions normally. Unfortunately, it does not stop there. The altered genetic makeup of the damaged cell causes replication of abnormal cells, predisposing the body to the development of cancer. And what is radiation but yet another form of *energy*?

In our example, radiation is powerful energy introduced into the body that affects the exposed cells by providing bad information directing them to produce diseased cells, leading to cancer formation. This is not dissimilar to a pet that is under the effects of negative energy from constant anger or conflict in the household environment. The negative energy patterns from the environment bombard the pet, and in time there is a potential for this energy to alter the pet's cellular function, thus creating physical (along with emotional) imbalance and disease. All we're really talking about is a difference in strength and concentration of the energy bombardment, but the function (and its result) is identical.

The Dimensions of Reality

Quantum scientists have theorized that there are as many as 11 dimensions that make up our reality (according to the M-theory pioneered by scientist Edward Witten). These dimensions each have their own energetic profile. The upper seven dimensions, imperceptible to us humans, exist so that the energy potential can be altered in a specific manner in order to create all energetic potential. Hence, pure potentiality of creation. We humans, limited by our sensory capabilities, can realize only the lower four dimensions. (Well, in truth we are fully aware of the lower three dimensions, but we are just starting to perceive the fourth—the combination of the three spatial dimensions with the addition of time—through the study of quantum physics.) Beyond this is where transition from the material to the nonmaterial occurs according to higher-dimensional mathematics. However, just because we cannot perceive the higher, nonmaterial dimensions with our senses does not mean that they do not exist. This is where quantum physics comes into play.

Let's use a very simple example: You turn on a radio, and there is nothing but static noise. You turn the dial a bit, and suddenly you are tuned in to a radio station that is playing a beautiful song. You move the dial a bit further and lose the song, but in short order you hear the voice of a man reading the latest news.

The sounds you pick up as you move the dial on the radio are being broadcast on different frequencies. The sound waves are always there whether or not you have tuned in to them. However, once you attune your radio's receiving frequency by changing the dial, it aligns with the frequency being broadcast, and the sound is manifested through the radio. As you turn the dial, the individual frequencies do not disappear, but the ability to perceive them is possible only when your radio is in alignment with that individual frequency.

Imagine the universe as a cosmic soup of wave patterns with endless potential. For simplicity, let's call this the highest dimension that exists. Then imagine that a portion of that same source is manipulated a bit to form energy. Although different, it is still made up of the original source energy. Once again, the new energetic dimension is manipulated a bit to form a new dimension of energy, and so on. Each dimension has its own energetic profile and function, yet it is still composed of the original source energy. As this process continues, the energetic manipulation alters the appearance of the energy itself until it reaches a dimension where it takes on a physical form as matter—what we call the third dimension. Some people describe this process as the energy getting denser.

The point is, even though this energetic dimension now has a physical form and function, it is still composed of the original source energy derived from the highest dimension. As far as we currently understand according to quantum physics, this is how the physical body—along with all physical existence in our universe—is formed.

Because our physical body exists at the lower three dimensions, our consciousness or awareness is also at this lower dimension—and our sense as a separate, individual self necessarily limits our perception of the greater consciousness.

However, since the dawn of our species, we humans have had a sense of something greater than us pulling the strings.

So let's run with that for a moment. From this perspective, it's clear that the highest dimension (whatever you want to call it—be it God, source energy, or the Universe) is always fully aware of its own dimension and those below it, because it's driving this bus we call reality. But the reverse is not true. The lower dimensions are not aware of the higher ones when limited by the functions of the mind and its perceived realities. That radio simply doesn't pick up those frequencies. The only way that a lower dimension can become aware of a higher one is if it is raised to a higher level of consciousness (or frequency). Like energy perceives like energy.

Understanding how energetic dimensions work is imperative to understanding how the physical body can become distorted or imbalanced, producing disease. The medical profession and its Newtonian scientific methodologies have become stagnant in explaining health and healing. As long as medicine works within the boundaries of the lower dimensions, then we will be at the mercy of untreatable diseases, high costs for available treatments, and limited options for healing.

To put it more simply, broadening our perspective to the holistic view, which includes the higher dimensions, opens us up to new possibilities that will explain body function and healing, but we may not ever be able to measure those explanations in a laboratory. We must accept the limitations of the reductionist logic of the physical dimension, without being bound by them.

To paraphrase Albert Einstein, "You will never answer the question at the same energetic dimension that created the question." You must move to a higher level of thinking—a higher dimension—in order to understand the problem and find the ultimate answer.

What Really Controls Bodily Function (and Dysfunction)

To understand a theory of healing *dysfunction,* we have to first understand *normal* function. The important thing to remember is that although we and our pets are limited in our perceptions and our awareness, the source of the information that will guide us in form and function—the plan for our energetic potential to be converted to our genetic components—lies outside the physical body in another energetic dimension. This higher-dimension source is aware of us at the lower dimensions and has complete control of our form and function. It is what initiates and maintains function, directs regeneration of tissue, and begins healing. Remember the flock of birds flying in harmony as if being directed by something outside their little bodies? The same scenario applies to the cells of the body.

Let's look now at how we can apply our new understanding of the body's energetic makeup to health and healing—starting with how the body becomes energetically imbalanced. Imagine that the energetic source that flows through the body has information that controls its function so that its normal existence is well-being and harmony, at all times directing it toward health and happiness. The only way this will change is if there is something that interferes with this energetic flow or alters its character. Once the energetic flow is altered or obstructed, the physical manifestation will be imbalance, disease will develop, and symptoms will appear. Healing is simply *removing the resistance or obstruction* to the natural pathway and allowing the flow of well-being to return.

In his book *Analog Medicine: A Science of Healing,* veterinarian Ronald Hamm compares the body's energetic field to that of a magnetic field. He instructs the reader to imagine placing a piece of paper over a magnet and sprinkling metal filings on the paper. The filings will form a physical image of the magnetic pattern, much like that of the energetic body. Now, if you move the filings around with your finger, the pattern will be distorted. However, if you remove your finger, the filings will return to their original arrangement, dictated by the field of the magnet. This is how the body heals. Simply remove the resistance or obstruction of the energy flow, and the body will return to its original form and function.

Treating Disease in the Lower Dimensions

Let's look at another hypothetical example. Pluto is a middle-aged terrier that has developed a small lump on his neck. Minnie, Pluto's caretaker, notices the lump and takes him to see his veterinarian, who takes a biopsy of the tissue to send to the laboratory. In a couple of days, the report states that the lump is a grade 3 mast cell tumor, a malignancy that has the potential to spread to other parts of the body, ultimately leading to Pluto's death. The veterinarian recommends immediate surgical removal, as well as a biopsy of the regional lymph node to see if the cancer has spread to the nearest location.

Pluto returns for surgery, the lump is removed, and the regional lymph node is biopsied. Several days later, the latest report comes back, indicating that there are cancer cells in the lymph node as well. The veterinarian calls Minnie in for a consultation and recommends that Pluto begin chemotherapy treatment since the cancer has already spread to other parts of the body. Minnie is told that chemotherapy is the only option for Pluto if the cancer is to be further treated.

Minnie loves Pluto and has the financial ability to afford the chemotherapeutic regime. Pluto begins the treatment, although Minnie has been told that the prognosis for survival even with chemotherapy is very poor.

This is a classic example of diagnosing and treating a disease at the lower dimensions of the physical body, and it's what most of us are familiar with. But perhaps Minnie becomes aware of a veterinarian who integrates complementary modalities into his practice, and asks him for a second opinion. Pluto is evaluated from an energetic perspective, and the treatment protocol is to reestablish a balance and the proper flow of energy.

Instead of zeroing in on the grade 3 mast cell tumor as the disease, the new veterinarian focuses on the energetic imbalances. He offers a combination of acupuncture and Chinese herbs. Remembering that the upper dimensions always include the lower ones, the veterinarian knows that treating Pluto from the higher-dimension, energetic perspective will affect the lower, physical dimension as well. If the healing is successful, there is a high probability that not only will the energetic imbalances and movements be corrected, but the mast cell tumor in the physical dimension will also be resolved.

Unfortunately, the reverse does not work. Even if the tumor is successfully treated at the physical level using science-based Western medicine, its underlying energetic cause has not been addressed. There remains a probability that the tumor will return.

Treating Disease in the Higher Dimensions

Energy-working healers understand the significance of dimensional energy, as it helps uncover the source of an imbalance that has created a disease. They begin their attention at the level of the physical body and collect information pertaining to issues such as nutritional imbalances, toxicities, and infections. Then they move into a higher energetic dimension and collect information regarding mental and emotional disturbances—where sensitive healers find that most chronic diseases affecting the physical body originate. (We'll discuss this more in Chapter Nine, "Complementary Modalities.") Finally, they move to the higher dimensions of the spirit, searching for imbalances that originate there. Once the sources are located, healing is directed by focusing intention on removing the root causes.

Clinicians who are aware of how healing actually works understand, first and foremost, that *they* are not the ones responsible for the healing. Remember, from the energetic perspective, they are simply helping remove blockages or imbalances so the system can right itself. The "action" is taking place at the higher dimensions, which inform the lower, physical dimensions. When healing occurs in this manner, it is unlikely that the disease will return.

On the other hand, Western medicine approaches disease as though it is a force separate from the body that must be attacked and eradicated. This is one of the great paradoxes of chemotherapy as a treatment for cancer. Chemotherapy is used to destroy cancer cells, but most of the time the therapy cannot distinguish between them and normal cells, hence the severe side effects. There's no denying that Western medicine cures many people, but collateral damage seems inherent in this approach. With the help of the pharmaceutical industry, we've come to accept this collateral damage as the norm, perhaps even at the price of health and well-being. But as I said in the very beginning of this book, my goal is to help shift what we accept as the norm.

How many more people and pets could we heal—*for good,* without recurrence—if our approach included awareness of and working with the higher dimensions as a complement to healing on the lower dimensions?

The Essence of the Individual

Imagine source energy as a sea of unlimited possibilities. For this dimension to begin its creative process, there has to be a directed focus, called an intention, that can activate the universal source. Intention by definition requires awareness or conscious thought—a desire to *create* something. My belief, and that of many holistic practitioners, is that the source energy or something that energy is part of . . . is the sea of potentiality itself.

Intention activates universal laws that initiate the flow of energy from higher to lower dimensions. Ultimately, the energetic body is created, and as the energy is altered, mass is created in the form of atoms and molecules. Biochemicals are formed, and then cells. The higher-dimensional energy is coded into the genetic blueprint of the cells, and each cell follows its instructions to create the various parts of the body, giving form and function. The inherited information from the higher energetic dimensions controls the development, maintenance, and regeneration of the physical body.

Each animal, plant, and mineral thus has an individual energetic makeup often referred to as its *essence* or its *authentic self.* Created by a divine plan with a divine purpose, this essence is expressed as a harmonious flow of energy and information that is unlike anything else that has ever been created and, at the same time, with a connectedness to all energy fields. In this state, the individual expresses well-being and alignment of body, mind, and spirit—perfect balance—like the natural flow of a stream, moving along in harmony with its purpose.

The problems arise when there is a blockage or resistance in that energetic flow, akin to a fallen tree partially blocking the flow of the stream, forcing it to divert its energy. A new bend in the river or a sharp, cutting bank might develop. The same happens with the body; some form of resistance might block the natural flow of energy, and a new expression may occur.

This resistance could take the form of a toxin or infection that affects the body at the physical level, or it could be due to emotional or mental disturbances. Any resistance, at any energetic dimension, can alter the manifestation of the normal flow of energy and information to the body, and consequently imbalance and disease may occur. Removing the energetic resistance or obstruction will reestablish the natural flow of the divine expression, which is well-being.

As an example, let's look at nervous-tissue damage and loss of function. According to Western medicine, nervous tissue does not have regenerative abilities and is incapable of healing. A spinal cord that has been extensively damaged due to a traumatic event is considered functionally "dead," and paralysis results. A Western-trained veterinary clinician gives the patient a poor prognosis based on his education, beliefs, and experiences. The patient's caretaker now believes that the paralysis is permanent—based on *his* recent education and experience—and that his beloved pet will most likely be confined to some sort of mechanical assistance for movement, such as a cart.

However, the holistic practitioner understands that there has been an obstruction along the energetic pathway that creates form and function of the spinal cord, like the tree that has fallen into the stream and temporarily disrupted its normal flow or expression. The holistic clinician may opt to use modalities that will relieve the energetic resistance and reestablish the flow's original expression. Physically, the spinal cord returns to its normal form and function.

It is difficult for a veterinarian not trained in energy medicine to understand how a dog with a ruptured disk causing mechanical obstruction of the spinal cord can heal without physically removing the disk. Yet all the factors involved in this disease process (spinal cord, disk, and so on) are composed of energy, which can be manipulated to return to its original state. Acupuncture, Chinese herbs, Reiki, and Reconnective Healing are just a few modalities that could be used to reestablish the spinal cord's energetic field.

Keeping Intention in Mind

Understanding the power of energetic modalities to establish well-being and harmony is a giant step toward understanding healing. They also give us options that might minimize the use of traditional Western medicine such as harmful chemicals or invasive surgery. However, we must remember that, though treatments are focused on the energetic body, *healing is initiated at an even higher dimension*. Moreover, it can only be initiated by an *intention* to heal.

Once the intention is established, the process of manifestation requires focus and belief. Nothing more is necessary: not needles, drugs, surgery, or even herbs. We use these to help us *focus* our intention sufficiently. The world's greatest healers have the ability to concentrate solely on a healing intention, but it's not something most of us can do without the help of tools and methodologies. Still, the fact remains that universal laws will result in healing when intention, focus, and belief are present and tuned in to the natural flow of energy from source (the highest dimension) all the way through to the body (the lower, physical dimension).

Fewer than half the people who regularly take something for a headache properly metabolize the pills in a way that could be healing for them. This is a powerful everyday example of the placebo effect at work. You can see it all around you, probably in your own life. But all those people still need the pill to cure their headache. They've *focused* their *intention* on the headache going away; they *believe* the pill will heal them. All three criteria are present. The pill is merely the tool that allows them to get out of their own way so healing can occur.

Now imagine that you aren't feeling well and go to a doctor, who does a thorough examination and makes a diagnosis: You have a malignant cancer. Immediately, you are going to react to the words *malignant cancer.* Your reaction is a deep and emotionally charged one, based solely on your experience of cancer. The story you've told yourself throughout your life is that malignant cancer is bad and will most likely lead to suffering and death. If the *doctor* tells you that the cancer will likely lead to suffering and death, your story will be reinforced and your belief will become stronger.

Let's say that instead the doctor tells you that you have a simple infection. Your automatic response will be quite different, since the story you've told yourself about simple infections is much different than the one about malignant cancer. The doctor's prognosis aligns with your story, and you're convinced that after a round of antibiotics, the infection will be eliminated.

In each situation, you have a physical condition (the cancer or infection) and a nonphysical belief or story. And in each situation, your belief is reinforced and you are left with an expectation. Energetically speaking, that belief is a critical piece of the puzzle.

In the case of the simple infection, the intent to return to normal health was created. The focus was on the use of antibiotics: Each time you took them, you further reinforced your belief that the infection was simple, the antibiotics would eliminate it, and normal health would return.

In the case of the malignant cancer, the pieces of the puzzle work the same way. The intent originates as a hope to return to normal health. But the belief about the outcome—which is the result of the story you've told yourself, exacerbated by the doctor's prognosis—has created a different expectation. The focus is, yet again, on the use of treatment aimed at eliminating the condition, but it is inhibited by the belief that the outcome will be suffering and death.

Sustained healing cannot occur without the *expectation* of healing, no matter the form of treatment. The culmination of your beliefs creates your reality, which reinforces those beliefs, and the cycle continues. That is, *until you change your beliefs.*

Healing is simply allowing yourself to fulfill your—or your pet's—destiny of well-being through your focus, intention, and belief.

How Energy Alters Itself . . . and Can *Be* Altered

Energy patterns take the form of wave frequencies measured in units called hertz (Hz). These are the same units used in electrical energy as well as electromagnetic energy. Centuries ago a Dutch scientist named Christiaan Huygens (1629–1695) discovered that if he placed two pendulum clocks close to each other and started the pendulum at opposite positions, in time they would synchronize and swing in unison. We call this phenomenon *entrainment.* It occurs when different frequencies lock into phase with one another in an attempt to become more efficient. Energetically speaking, it is easier to cooperate than to oppose forces. That is how energy finds harmony.

Entrainment occurs whenever two dissimilar energies come together—whether within the body, between bodies, or within higher organizations of energy such as society. The energetic body is constantly coming in contact with "unlike" energy and is subject to the properties of entrainment. (A good example is when several women come together, and over a period of time their menstrual cycles become synchronous.)

Within the physical body, there are many vibrational energy patterns occurring all the time. The heart and brain have been studied for years with the use of electrocardiogram (EKG) and electroencephalogram (EEG) equipment, which measure electrical wave frequencies and patterns in these organs. Research by neuroscientists has led to categorization of brain-wave patterns and their effects on the physical body. The higher-vibrational electricity patterns that occur during the brain's beta state are typically what we experience day to day with our high-stress, busy lives. In time, the persistence of higher beta states leads to physical exhaustion and imbalance that may manifest in disease.

Knowing how energetic states react with one another, we can use energy-altering techniques—meditation and prayer are good examples—that will move the brain's electricity patterns into an alpha state: one that is lower in frequency and will help relieve exhaustion and stress. This also is why rest reinvigorates the physical body. During sleep, the brain often enters lower-frequency brain-wave patterns such as alpha, delta, or theta. These lower-frequency patterns have a rebalancing effect that aids in healing.

Veterinary and medical clinicians who incorporate energy-healing modalities use energy principles to similarly reestablish balance within the physical body.

The rational mind, the brain's left hemisphere, gets most of its input from the five senses. When a patient is examined, the clinician begins receiving input and within just a few minutes, the reasoning mind begins its job of evaluation and determines what will most likely be the answer. At that time, the brain will no longer receive input from the senses, opting to "cut to the chase" in solving the problem. Because the energetic body is not perceived by the human senses, and the rational brain will not receive this input automatically, clinicians must use other techniques to assess the energy health of their patients. Here are a few examples:

- **Pulse diagnosis** can evaluate the energetic pulse of the patient, or the clinician when in contact with the patient.

- **Acupuncture meridians or acupuncture points** can assess energy flow or any excesses and deficiencies of energy.

- **Computer technology** can analyze the patient's energetic profile to aid the clinician.

- **The "analog mind"** also offers a unique assessment approach. Some clinicians are able to place themselves into a state of mind in which they become sensitive to their patient's energy field. The input comes as a passive awareness through meditation, focus, or prayer. (In *Analog Medicine,* Dr. Hamm calls this the "analog mind"—the part of the mind that is aligned with interconnectedness, compassion, empathy, and love.)

Clinicians who use energy medicine know that they will have to come into alignment with the patient by turning off the reasoning portion of the brain and energetically connecting to the individual.

At that time, they may be able to detect imbalance in the energy field or blockage of energy flow.

Once the energetic assessment of the patient has been done, *then* clinicians will switch into rational modes of reasoning to derive a treatment plan. The plan will be successful in promoting healing only if it addresses methods to reestablish the patient's energetic balance and normal energy flow.

By now, you might feel a bit overwhelmed by all this new information. Let me take a moment to give you a simple context for what you have learned about how our bodies, and our pets' bodies, function as part of the energetic dance going on within and around us all the time.

As you now understand, the physical body is the final product of cascading energetic events that originate in the higher, nonphysical dimensions. The body's manifestation, maintenance, and regeneration, as well as its healing capabilities, are likewise initiated in the higher, nonphysical dimensions of reality. We can opt to approach the physical body's health and harmony with traditional science-based perspectives that focus only on the lower energetic dimensions—but, as we've seen, these methods are inherently limited. Fortunately, we have the option to utilize this approach *while also* incorporating the higher dimensions, working with principles based on quantum physics and the subatomic world. By doing so, we can move right to the source —and work directly with those energies to expand our healing capabilities and holistic understanding of the physical body.

And so we bring all this new awareness back to the topic at hand, and nearest and dearest to our hearts—the health and well-being of our beloved pets.

CHAPTER FOUR

THE SPECIAL RELATIONSHIP BETWEEN PETS AND THEIR PEOPLE

*"Who can believe that there is no soul
behind those luminous eyes!"*

— THÉOPHILE GAUTIER

Claire was a six-year-old Doberman pinscher that was very ill when brought to the clinic. After a thorough examination, it became obvious with the aid of several laboratory tests that Claire's kidneys were failing, and her prognosis was very poor. I sat down with Claire's caretaker, Monique, and went over the bad news.

It was then that Monique explained that whenever she became ill, so did Claire. For instance, she would get an infection and, in a short while, so would Claire. Monique's tone was emphatic—she was convinced there was a connection between her health and Claire's. I told her that this was interesting information and I would take it into consideration.

I had just started my training in Traditional Chinese Medicine and veterinary acupuncture, and many things about the energetic world were still unknown to me. However, after three days in the clinic and receiving all that Western medicine had to offer, Claire continued to decline, so I decided to use alternative treatment in conjunction with traditional therapy.

Over the next couple of days, Claire seemed to improve. She started to get up and move around, and her persistent vomiting stopped. Soon after, she began to eat on her own, and in time she became stable enough to be sent home. Although repeated laboratory work indicated that her kidney function had not changed, she was obviously getting better. Over the next two months, Claire gained 20 pounds and, according to Monique, was acting like her old self. Six months later, Claire's kidneys failed again, and in just a matter of days, she died peacefully.

I had not thought about Claire in a while when the clinic receptionist told me that her caretaker had come in and wanted to see me in private. I walked into the exam room, and Monique started crying. Through the tears, she said, "I wanted to tell you that I was recently diagnosed with kidney failure, just like Claire."

Who among us doesn't feel a bit of tugging of our heartstrings when we hear a story like this? Animal lovers know that the relationships we develop with our pets are unique and incredibly special. And in embracing a holistic perspective, we realize that these relationships are truly multidimensional, and offer us great potential to learn about ourselves and how we interact with the rest of the world.

A Witness to Our Truth

It can be extremely difficult for us to grasp what we cannot experience with our physical senses—things like faith, love, and compassion that are not provable, yet that we know exist. We must *believe* in abstract concepts and then find the ways in which they express themselves at our level of consciousness. For example, when we show our pets gratitude, we know that the feeling overwhelming us at that moment is love. We believe, we experience, and then we *know.* This is why faith exists—so we can tap into the unprovable truths we can somehow *feel.* Then life presents us with opportunities to witness these truths in action.

The heart-to-heart energetic bond that exists between us and our beloved pets is one of these opportunities. It allows us to experience deep truths about ourselves. I have encountered so many friends and clients over the years who complained about their inability to commit to love and to give unconditionally, yet they wholeheartedly "commit" to their much-loved pet without realizing they are doing just that. Clients have told me that they didn't believe they were capable of being a "good" parent, but they gave of themselves totally when it came to their precious animals. They provided a loving, caring home, with an understanding of mutual dependence along with healthy boundaries. Could there be any better environment for a family?

Dr. Robin L. Smith, in her inspiring book *Hungry: The Truth About Being Full,* describes her loving relationship with her dog, Kalle. Shortly after Kalle's death, Robin was walking around her home feeling lonely, asking herself questions like, *How can I live without her? How can I bear the pain?*

Then Kalle's voice came to Robin. Her cherished dog said, "Mommy, if you take care of yourself the way that you took care of me, you'll be fine. If you don't, you're in big trouble."

So many times, in our attempt to give to our pets from a state of loving compassion, we forget to do the same for ourselves. Millions of people suffer from the misguided belief that they have no worth. They get wrapped up in a story about themselves based on past actions deemed inappropriate or bad, and believe they are unworthy of happiness. Then they go home to spend loving time with their pet, and the story fades for the moment. The heart-to-heart connection emerges, and joy abounds. In those moments, there are no stories— just the truth. Just love.

If we could only step back and watch ourselves expressing such love and compassion for our pets, then we might stop and say, "Wow, look at who I really am." We would witness ourselves as loving, caring human beings, and in time the experience would enable us to see the truth about ourselves. Our pets are certainly aware of this. You may have seen the bumper sticker that says, "God, help me be the person my dog thinks I am." It should say, "Thank you, God, for my pet, who allows me to witness the person that I really am."

The relationship we have with our pets is deeply reciprocal, and we benefit greatly by treating it as such and expanding our perspective. For instance, in most books about owning a pet, there is usually a chapter dedicated to selection, which covers information such as what type of pet you might consider—dog, cat, bird, and so on—and topics such as species characteristics, breeds, dispositions, and much more. These are all important considerations, but if we come from a holistic approach, we expand our minds to include and appreciate aspects of our animals that may not be covered in a conventional pet book, such as the larger awareness, truth, and heart-to-heart connection that our pets bring to our lives.

This applies to "ownership," too. In my opinion, the phrase *pet owner* is contrary to the word *holism.* It represents the body portion of the mind-body-spirit connection and therefore has a very limited perspective. Ownership reflects domination, and even though obtaining a pet certainly falls under the criteria of ownership, we must look upon it as beginning a relationship that may last for many years.

As you see, whether we are aware of it or not, *we* benefit from the relationship with our pet as much as the pet does. So, as *caretakers* of our animals, we appreciate the connection for so much more than simply an exchange of providing for our pet in return for some play time. As with the best of friendships, the relationship is a two-way street, and exists at a profoundly energetic level as well as a physical one.

An Energetic Connection

We all know people who love dogs, dislike cats, and wouldn't consider owning a bird or "pocket pet," such as a hamster or gerbil. But why do you think people have special interest in a particular type of pet? Why would someone select a Great Dane over a dachshund or a golden retriever over a Doberman? Why would someone be drawn to a feisty Siamese cat instead of a laid-back orange tabby? Are these random desires? Perhaps the preferential thoughts that come into our minds are actually little signposts directing us along a path that will connect us to that special pet that has a purpose for coming into our lives.

Most pet caretakers will agree that there is a special, unexplainable connection that exists between them and their animal companions, a sort of unconscious bond that cannot easily be put into words. There have been fascinating displays of this bond; for example, a man leaves the desk at his office, and immediately his dog at home jumps up and runs to the door. Or a cat rushes into the room and springs onto his caretaker's lap to notify her that she is about to suffer a seizure. This connection has been studied by many researchers, although at this time no one can explain it. In ways large and small, sensitive pet owners see this subtle but very real connection emerge.

For the type of response described in the examples above to occur, there must be at least two factors involved:

- An energetic connection between the pet and caretaker
- An awareness of that connection by at least one of the parties

All is energy—at a certain dimension, there is no differentiation between the pet and caretaker. In other words, the physical boundaries are removed. If one party (the pet) is aware of the energetic connection, then *it* will react energetically when the unaware party (the caretaker) alters itself energetically.

Why would an energy connection between pet and caretaker only be detected—and, therefore, acted on—by the pet? Remember our discussion about awareness from Chapter One, in which I explained how we can move between a broader, almost unfocused awareness where we are simply "being" and a specific, narrow focus that enables us to act on a practical level? Well, human beings are constructed to be hyperaware of our surroundings in order to interact with the material world we live in. We obtain information from our physical senses—sight, sound, touch, taste, and smell—and formulate a response in the brain. At least that is how scientists believe this happens.

Animals have the same five primary senses as humans, but they also have a sensitivity to *feelings* because they spend their time aware of everything that is happening in the moment. Because they are not distracted by a constant barrage of thoughts and concerns, our pets are, in a sense, more broadly aware than we are, and thus can perceive energy differently than we do. (If you want to see the ultimate Buddha, check out your pet.) It isn't that they sit there and think, *I am aware that my caretaker and I are connected.* They are simply *being aware.* Their internal radio is scanning all the stations all the time. They are thereby keenly tuned in to our emotions and are deeply affected by them, because at the energetic level there is no difference between them and us. I cannot state it often or clearly enough: From an energetic standpoint, *there are no physical boundaries.*

If we learn to quiet the perpetual mind chatter, then we open ourselves up to subtle messages that might come by way of thoughts or guidance. They might even arise in the form of energetic sensations emanating from our pets.

This is how animal communicators work with their clients. They have the ability to clear the noisy chatter from their minds and move into an awareness of the subtle energetic connection between them and the animal. The messages might come in the form of feelings, images, or words that the communicator can interpret. What appears to be a sensation of "receiving" information from an external source (the animal) is actually a sharing of the same energy.

Pets live close to their caretakers, and are thus receiving constant emotional energy from the shared environment. If the emotional health of the caretakers is good—filled with joy, happiness, and love—then the pet will thrive energetically. However, if there is an environment of fearful emotions—anger, depression, and anxiety—then the pet will suffer energetically. This concept is called *mirroring,* and it's a form of energy exchange.

This isn't just a fascinating fact; we can benefit *practically* from this knowledge as well. We now know that prolonged emotions, such as stress, can affect our bodies physically and lead to disorders such as immune suppression, heart disease, and cancer. If we accept that there is no energetic boundary between us and our pets, then we understand how the negative emotions that cause physical disease in *our* bodies, when carried into our environment, will cause physical disease in our pets as well. The story of Claire and Monique from the beginning of this chapter illustrates this phenomenon profoundly.

The Heart of the Matter

Several years ago at the HeartMath Institute—an organization in California whose mission is to help people "reduce stress, self-regulate emotions and build energy and resilience"—researchers were studying emotional effects on the human heart. In one experiment, a young boy and his dog were hooked up to instrumentation that would allow the researchers to assess the heart function of each and build a *cardiac profile* (a list of measured characteristics, such as heart rate and EKG statistics). The boy was then asked to display loving emotion to the dog. As one would expect, while he did so, the boy's heart function was *coherent* (a term given by researchers to indicate that the heart is functioning at maximum efficiency). However, when researchers looked at the *dog's* heart function, they were astonished to discover that not only was it coherent but both cardiac profiles were exactly the same. Energetically, the hearts became synchronized, and the energy was expressed in both physical hearts.

Further research at HeartMath has since proven not only that the *heart* is functioning at peak performance during cardiac coherence, but also that there appears to be maximum efficiency throughout the rest of the body. The researchers refer to this as *physiological coherence.* This implies that during periods when we are sharing loving emotions with our pets, our bodies (both ours and our pets') are functioning at maximum efficiency.

In my practice, I have taken this one step further. Caretakers with a sick or injured pet are instructed to administer loving attention once or twice a day. After spending a few minutes sharing affection, the caretakers are to visualize their pet in a state of perfect health. They might imagine their animal running and playing, happy and healthy. Caretakers who have been diligent in this practice have reported great success with it and seen vast improvements in health.

Comments such as "He hasn't been this energetic in years" or "She seems so much younger" are common.

I have witnessed relationships between pet and caretaker evolving in many ways over the years, which especially afford us caretakers myriad opportunities to learn about ourselves. No matter what is going on in the world that surrounds us, it is comforting to know that when we are with our pet, there is a depth of connection—a shared energetic bond—that we can always count on. We can escape the complexity of our thoughts and align ourselves with a truth that soothes the nervous mind. When we connect with our pets with loving, compassionate feelings, we can bypass the mind and enter into a consciousness in tune with the heart. It is during these times that we feel alive and free, away from life's burdens.

Our pets are a continuous source of alignment with truth. They remind us that life can be simple if we will remove ourselves from the "story" that constantly runs through our minds. Our pets are always happy, because they don't give meaning to everything that happens to them, like we tend to. If something negative occurs in the moment, they react by protecting themselves, then return to the next moment, without a story that connects them to the incident. This in no way means that our pets are simpleminded. On the contrary, they are inhabiting a state of mind that tackles situations as they are, without attaching a story.

By removing the story ourselves, we find the ability to connect to our inner self, where characteristics such as love, kindness, and compassion exist. Our pets can act as gentle everyday reminders of how life can be if we choose to live with grace in the moment. We might believe that our pets *make* us happy—but this is not the case. Rather, they lead us to rediscover our own happiness that comes from an inner, ever-present source. They remind us that feelings of joy are always available, and that we can move freely through our lives without depending on outside circumstances to bring us happiness. Our pets don't think, *Hey, I will be happy if my caretaker brings me a treat.* Instead, they display a flow of joy that moves from the inside out, bathing anything that is in their proximity in the truth that happiness exists in *all* of us.

Our pets offer us great opportunities to display qualities such as compassion, responsibility, patience, and kindness. They accept our flaws without judgment, love us unconditionally, and are faithful until the end, while asking absolutely nothing from us in return. Animals might show fear should we neglect them, but they will never stop loving us. They can't, because they *are* love and are fundamentally incapable of being anything other than pure source energy expressing itself.

I read a story about a fellow who died and was taken away to be buried. His dog, a male German shepherd, found his way to his caretaker's grave site, and for the next six months refused to leave. At no time had anyone taken the dog to the cemetery. The people who took care of the grounds adopted the dog and now feed and look after him, although he rarely leaves his caretaker's grave.

After reading this story, I asked myself, *What could explain this dog's purpose in sitting beside his caretaker's grave?* Perhaps the man's spirit still resides at the grave site, and his dog detects it. Or perhaps it is a blessed opportunity for us to witness true devotion.

A Doorway to Higher Dimensions

We and our pets spend most of our time in the third dimension—where energy is exhibited as physical matter—as well as in lower-energetic brain functions, such as thoughts and emotions. At the third dimension, we have the opportunity to explore all the wonders of our world and create thoughts and emotions that may help us navigate through our lives.

However, as I've previously explained, there are times when these energies can become imbalanced, which may lead to physical, mental, or emotional diseases. If negative emotional states become our norm, they will keep us grounded deeply in the third dimension. We can feel the "heaviness" of these energies—when we speak of the weight of depression or sadness, for example, we are talking about the sensation of heavy energies.

When we are experiencing periods of joy, then, we are elevating ourselves *beyond* the third dimension. The fourth dimension consists of lighter energy, which makes us feel good and confident of ourselves. As we move into higher dimensions of energy, we take on new perspectives and shed constrictions of lower dimensions; we experience the unity of all things. Unfortunately, we all too often find ourselves slipping back into the lower dimension.

Let's look at an example. Maybe you just spent time out in the park playing with your dog and enjoying the beautiful day. When you return home, you feel light and energetic. This is because you have taken your energetic self to the higher fourth dimension. Later that day, you start thinking about what you have to do tomorrow. Suddenly, you find yourself worrying about your job, bills, and so on. The heavy energetic patterns of worry, stress, and anxiety have lowered your overall energetic balance so that it can no longer exist at the level of the fourth dimension. You have just let yourself slip back into the third dimension.

When we find ways to spend more time in the higher dimensions—those above the third dimension—our lives become more joyous, more secure, and more aligned with our natural well-being. To function in the world, we necessarily must spend *some* time in the third dimension, of course. But as we've seen, when it comes to energy, it's all about *balance.* If we are aware of how energy works and how we are affected by it, then we can look for ways to keep ourselves in the higher dimensions for longer periods to balance out what we experience in the lower dimensions. This will benefit our minds, bodies, and spirits.

When we are focused on our busy, stressful lives, we are grounded in the third dimension, and we struggle without answers. The only way to break those patterns is to learn to move ourselves into the higher energetic dimensions, where guidance comes to us freely and naturally. There are many ways to do so—*and one is via our energetic connection to our pets.* When we spend time with our beloved pets and focus on our loving affection for them, we *automatically* connect with our higher level of consciousness; the obstructions and resistances produced in the lower dimensions are removed, and we obtain clarity. And what is amazing is how effortless and joyful it is to do so.

From this perspective, we may open doors that we have been desperately looking for. Maybe we have been struggling with a decision to change jobs or move on from a current relationship. At the lower, third dimension, we attempt to answer these questions by using our rational minds and get lost in the thought process of *Is this right or is this wrong?* When we move ourselves into the fourth dimension, we can focus on the present moment, remove our busy mind chatter, feel our joy as we spend time with our beloved pet, and wait until guidance comes. And when it does, it comes like the wind, unforced and unannounced.

Communicating with Your Pet

We can derive other benefits from our awareness of the energetic bond between us and our pets. One is a new ability to communicate.

Have you ever wondered how animal communicators converse with animals? They weren't born with a unique God-given talent. Animal communicators will be the first to admit that *anyone* can learn to communicate with their pets. We can learn to do this through our awareness of that energetic connection we share with our animals.

Animals communicate with each other by several means, but one of the methods is directly linked with their brain function. Unlike most human beings, animals are dominated by their intuitive brain, or what some people call the right hemisphere. When right-brain dominance exists, the pet experiences an awareness of the interconnection of all beings. This level of consciousness allows him or her to know the intentions of others. Some refer to this as telepathic communication, while others call it extrasensory perception (ESP).

Imagine your dog is out in the backyard watching the birds on the power line. He is in the moment, and his mind is focused on the birds. But he is also aware of the telepathic communication between the other members of his pack (you, plus members of the family) and him. Suddenly, he picks up an intention that you are getting ready to leave. Immediately, he shifts his focus from his sense-dominated brain (watching the birds) to your intention, and he responds by running into the house and begging to go with you.

How many times have you approached your pet with the intention of taking him to the veterinary clinic or to the grooming shop, and he knew what your intentions were and nervously scurried away? Some people believe that he sensed your deception or smelled your pheromone release, but in *truth* it was his inherent ability to communicate with you telepathically that warned him of your intention. This is why you might not be able to find your cat when you need to take her to the veterinarian. She determines your intention long before you take action and safely hides under a bed or in the neighbor's garden.

You may wonder why our pets have this unique ability to communicate with each other and with us, while we don't have the ability. The truth is—we *do.* However, our minds are so preoccupied with survival, left brain–type activity, that we lose our ability to communicate at a deeper level of consciousness. If we teach ourselves to focus on our breathing and quiet our mind chatter, we can shift our awareness from left brain to right brain, meeting our pets' consciousness where it lives and perceiving the subtle energy coming from them at all times.

Since the "mindful mind" does not communicate in the same manner as the rational brain, we must open ourselves to anything that might appear. The communication from our pet might come in the way of images, feelings, or thoughts instead of words. But if we stay focused on receiving the information and don't analyze it (which moves us back into the left-brain function and stops the communication), then we can collect it and, if need be, analyze what it means later, when we are back in left-brain mode. In time and with practice, communicating with our pets may be more effective than communicating with our teenage children!

When we open ourselves to this remarkable channel of communication with our pets, we can move into understanding them in ways we've never imagined. So many times we admit that if we *only knew* what they were trying to say to us, we would know what to do. Perhaps they are attempting to warn us of an impending danger; or maybe they are gravely ill, and we would like to find out if they are ready to transition. Animal communicators have been a blessing for me and other pet owners, as they have guided us through very troubling times by allowing us to understand the pet's perspective on the situation.

Using Visualization to Connect

You don't have to accept the illusion of boundaries. They're self-imposed, and they don't exist. You can change your beliefs by using your imagination and visualizing what it would be like in your ideal world—and then get really excited about this becoming reality. How happy would you be if you, your pets, and everyone you love were in a constant state of well-being? Can you imagine that? If so, then start creating . . .

As I mentioned, I frequently instruct my clients to use visualization to promote their pets' healing. I tell them to find a quiet place, connect with their mindful state of being, and visualize their animal companion playing in a serene environment while manifesting perfect health. You can do this, too, and you don't need to wait until an illness manifests.

Create a daily practice, perhaps while you are relaxed and enjoying your pet's company, of visualizing you both happy, healthy, and in perfect alignment through nonverbal connection. See your relationship the way you would like it to be. Reinforce your visualizations with the intention for your vision to be reality . . . and it will eventually become so.

Imagination is a powerful force, as it starts the dynamic process of creation. Everything humans have ever created in this physical world began as an idea derived from imagination. Imagination has to be the precursor of ideas, as it is the only way that we can think rationally without the impediments of our physical senses. It is a direct link to our higher consciousness and is a wonderful tool that we can use to aid in creation.

If we use our minds to imagine our pets in a state of well-being, then the process of creating healing has begun. We don't even have to figure out *how* this will happen. It is not our job. We might be instructed to participate in the process, and when we have done our part, we can sit back and enjoy the expectation of well-being expressing itself.

We all have imagination. Children, however, are the real experts. They imagine and pretend as naturally as they breathe. This is their reality. Unfortunately, most of us have diminished the importance of using our imagination, and thus it has atrophied. For example, I have heard countless people ask, "How can I know that God exists?" I remember when I first asked my wonderful minister the same question. This lovely lady said, "If you don't truly believe, then pretend. There is no reason not to. Pretend that God exists and imagine how your world would be if you knew this. Then your reality will *prove* to you that God does exist." In other words, we can't *know,* but we can *imagine*, and with our imagination, we can *create* reality. It is that simple.

Great Responsibility, Great Potential

When animal communicators ask pets what they require from us humans who cross paths with them, they tend to respond in the same manner: "Love me." Such a simple way to characterize such a rich dynamic! But those are animals for you. With an existence rooted in a constant state of presence and connectedness, they are the true Zen masters.

The relationships we develop with our pets are an interdimensional experience that, as should be very clear by now, bestows on us an incredible responsibility, even as it offers us great potential for our own personal growth and a deeper understanding of our true selves. I'm sure you can understand why the depth of this responsibility goes well beyond feeding your pet nutritiously, ensuring that she is up-to-date on her shots, making certain he has enough exercise, and so on—though we will cover those aspects of care in this book, too, because they are important pieces of the puzzle. But we are just beginning to explore the potential and the opportunities that a heart-to-heart bond with a pet can open to us. Let's move on to Part II, "Caring for Your Pet Holistically," to continue the journey.

PART II

CARING FOR YOUR PET HOLISTICALLY

CHAPTER FIVE

A NEW PERSPECTIVE ON HEALING, CURING, AND SUFFERING

"Although the world is full of suffering,
it is also full of the overcoming of it."

— HELEN KELLER

To offer our pets the best holistic care possible, we need to make a choice. It's not necessarily, above all, choosing the right veterinarian, selecting the right diet, or finding the right remedies for our animal companions—though all these things are important and discussed in detail in this section, Part II. The choice we first and foremost need to make is to *internally shift,* actually, in order to gain a new perspective on healing, curing, and suffering, and what they truly mean. In that sense, this chapter will be a gateway into the ones that follow, and it will offer a solid foundation for how you approach caring for your pet.

Let's begin with an example. Say your pet gets a thorn in her paw. If this happens, she has a physical disease; in veterinary medicine, we call it a "foreign body in the pad." And if you remove the thorn from the paw without incident, you have cured the disease. Pretty simple.

To *cure* something or somebody is the simple act of removing the disease, such as the thorn. The word *cure* comes from the Latin *cura,* meaning "to care." In medical terms, it is defined as "the return to normal health." Today, in medicine, our primary goal is to cure the patient so that he or she can return to normal function.

Healing is not the same as curing, however.

Merriam-Webster's Collegiate Dictionary defines *heal* as "to make whole; to cause to be overcome; to restore to original purity or integrity." The definition itself implies that healing goes a bit "deeper" than curing. It seems to indicate that healing is a restoration of a state of being that was meant to be. It might not make a difference when it comes to removing a thorn in a pet's paw or perhaps treating a lower urinary tract infection with antibiotics and eliminating the patient's symptoms. But if there is no response to treatment, or if symptoms recur, then curing may not get "deep" enough to return the patient back to the natural state of well-being.

If we look at individual diseases from a Western perspective, focusing on the ability to cure the patient, then we can get pretty close to determining the outcome of each disease using research and statistics. Some, historically, respond well to treatment, and a cure is quite predictable. Others don't respond as favorably, and the probability of finding a cure diminishes. Then there are those diseases that historically respond poorly to treatment and are labeled "incurable." They might not result in death, but invariably the symptoms will persist, despite all attempts with known treatments. Degenerative diseases, such as arthritis and dementia, fall into this category. The doctor usually tells us that there is little hope for a cure and that we will have to settle for treatments aimed at a reduction of clinical symptoms.

Healing is different. Healing may include curing, but it may not. Patients who have been cured of cancer only to have the cancer return years later were cured at the time—that is, they returned to normal health—but they are no longer, as their symptoms have come back. What is crucial to know is that healing *may have occurred* while the patient was being cured, and although the cancer has returned, the patient might still be healed. How is this possible? It has to do with a plan that is larger than us, larger than our physical existence, which we will discuss in depth in this chapter.

So, to make the distinction, curing is usually associated with the physical body, but it can include mental and emotional diseases as well. Healing, on the other hand, is not limited to the physical body, thoughts, or emotions. Healing deals with higher-energy states than those of the body.

If I am presented with a cat that has white fur and blue eyes, I know there is a high probability that the animal will have hearing deficiencies. This is because, genetically, the cat has developed without certain capacities of the inner ear required for normal hearing. Medicine describes these diseases as genetic disorders. Down syndrome in humans is another example.

If a deaf, white-haired, blue-eyed cat comes to the clinic with a skin infection, and I successfully treat the infection, is the cat cured even though she is still deaf? Of course—the cat has been returned to her original state of being, which in this case includes deafness.

Every individual—human or animal—has a divine plan that leads him or her down an individual pathway. The deaf cat has a divine plan that includes deafness. This divine plan or pathway will not be changed no matter what we attempt to do in order to alter it, and we may never understand the reasoning behind it, as that is beyond the ability of our rational mind. But with awareness, through allowing and accepting our divine plan, we find true healing.

The Power of Storytelling

Every day across the U.S., hundreds of precious cats are diagnosed with chronic renal failure. From a Western-medicine perspective, this means that the cat's kidneys are no longer capable of doing their job. Sometimes the cause of the kidney damage might be found, and once resolved with proper treatment, all returns to normal. However, most of the time, this does not happen. The caretaker is told that the cat's kidneys are incapable of resuming normal function. A therapeutic plan is devised that will help support the kidneys and minimize clinical symptoms for as long as possible. This might include a diet change, fluid support (with intermittent fluid therapy under the cat's skin or in the vein), medication to eliminate the nausea associated with kidney failure, and other medications determined by the veterinarian. The prognosis for the kidneys, and the life expectancy of the cat, is then communicated to the caretaker. (Determining the prognosis is dependent on multiple factors.)

If we as caretakers are faced with this scenario, all of the above is part of the *story* that our veterinarian has told to us, which we have chosen to accept. As we might expect, this story—that the kidneys will not return to normal function, that there is nothing more to do except offer support, and that our pet will eventually die from this disease—generates an emotionally charged response in us . . . and, typically, another story. Immediately, most of us will conjure up in our minds what the future will look like. This creates yet more negatively charged emotions, and the cycle continues.

We are creating stories about a future that is absolutely unknown, and in doing so we suffer. Then we share our stories with family and friends, and they, being loving, compassionate beings, sympathize with us and reinforce all the reasons why we should be suffering. Suddenly, we have an environment filled with well-meaning, emotionally suffering people, who are energetically influencing the enlightened cat—the cat that is always in the present moment, not telling himself a story at all.

The cat is simply *being,* and in that moment of being, the cat's kidneys are diseasing, nothing more. He doesn't mope around telling himself that he's dying and that this disease is "not fair" and should not be his lot. If the cat doesn't have an appetite, he is fasting. If he is vomiting, he is vomiting. Once the vomit reflex stops, then he is no longer vomiting. Maybe the medications will help the cat's appetite, and then he will be eating instead of fasting. *That's all.* No stories about what is going on.

So why is it that we humans are so engrossed in *our* stories, while our pets don't create them at all?

Stories arise at the time in our consciousness when we believe we become separate individuals. Until that time, we—like our pets—are not self-conscious, and we live in complete acceptance. This is a state of being. We have no stories, so we have no wants, no desires, and no goals, nothing beyond complete acceptance of being. We still become aware of being hungry, being tired, being in pain, and so on.

But nothing in our minds tells us a story that it should or shouldn't be happening.

Then, when we get old enough, someone explains to us that we are a separate being, and we listen and believe. From that time forward, we look at every situation and attempt to control the outcome to favor us as an individual. We spend the rest of our lives seeking control over fear and setting up situations that will allow us to experience pleasure.

Our pets never develop this self-awareness or sense of separation. Like children, they still respond to needs and still experience being in the moment. But there is no story that leads them into a situation, no story during it, and no story after the event is over. They move from one state of being to the next.

When there is no ego mind constantly telling stories, from that quietness proceeds intuition—the information that comes to us that we *know* is true. We don't question it. It is the guiding force that moves us along our pathway. Some refer to this as "moving in the flow of things." It is only when the busy mind interferes and creates confusion that we disconnect from our intuition. Buddhists teach that if we focus on the moment in quietness, intuition will arise, leading to insight. This is the direction back to truth. This is where our pets reside. This is why they are enlightened beings.

It is hard for us to understand how this can be, as it is entirely different from our accustomed *actions* and *reactions,* in which our minds immediately activate and start telling us what, why, and so on. Then off we go trying to listen to this story in order to regain control. Pets, however, never experience loss of control, and they live in complete harmony with the events that occur, never asking why. When pain arises, they feel it come and act accordingly. They have a natural response that tells them to relax into the pain, stay still. Then the pain subsides, and they are back in their natural state of being, one of joy.

Healing begins when we understand that suffering occurs only in our minds. Healing is aligning with that truth. Nonhealing is telling ourselves a story that is not aligned with truth. Then we experience fear. For example, we know that we are all dying, one day at a time. No matter what we do to extend our life expectancy, ultimately death will find us. There is no "cure," and the inevitability of death frightens many of us, driving much of the suffering that has become part of the human condition.

But we can "heal" ourselves with respect to death. If we can accept the truth that death is part of our divine plan—if we can embrace it rather than tell ourselves stories that fool us into thinking we can avoid it or control it when it occurs—then we will enter a divine state of mind that eliminates the fear. This is healing. It is that simple.

Why Pets Don't Really Suffer

The good news is that our pets don't suffer. The bad news is that *we* do. Sure, pets experience pain and display symptoms of diseases, but they don't suffer. Suffering comes when we tell ourselves stories about the disease. Since our pets don't tell themselves stories, they don't suffer.

Many times clients have said, "My dog is in pain, and he is suffering." But it isn't true. What *is* true is that your dog has pain, and *you* are suffering. Your dog is not saying to himself, *Oh my, I am in pain. My pain won't allow me to go outside and play with my caretaker. That makes me so unhappy.* No, your dog is just being. He is completely present and connected to the natural flow of energy all around him, accepting whatever unfolds. At one moment in time, there might be pain and he will express it. Then, in the next moment, he might not.

When a veterinarian tells you that your pet has cancer and that she is expected to live for only another six months, he is telling you *his* story. Then you immediately create your own, and the suffering begins. Your pet might have cancer, and she *might* die within six months, but I assure you that she will not suffer during this time. Your pet lives in an awareness of being, and that state of being is aligned with her divine plan. She never strays from that state of consciousness, and therefore suffering does not occur.

Suffering occurs only when we align our story with something that is not true. When we tell ourselves that our pet "shouldn't" have cancer, we are attempting to convince ourselves that her state of being is not aligned with the divine plan. In doing so, we deny the truth and, consequently, we suffer. When we accept the truth—that our pet has cancer and that there are no mistakes in truth—we begin to heal, and the suffering stops. Then we can make treatment decisions from a higher perspective, we can be there for her completely, and we can love her unconditionally. We will not be hung up on the emotions of fear and suffering.

When we get caught up in the battle against truth and allow suffering to occur, we move ourselves into a state of being that is not healthy for us *or* our pet. Our energetic profile diminishes to a denser, heavier state of being, and we not only predispose ourselves to un-healthy emotions and thoughts but also set ourselves up for physical imbalances and disease. We expose our pet, who is already physically and energetically imbalanced, to negative energy patterns that fur-ther inhibit the body's normal ability to cure itself.

In much the same way, turning our awareness to emotional and spiritual ease can help *heal* the physical body. When we focus on higher-dimensional healing, often a physical cure arises at the same time. Even if the diseased body is *not* cured, when we obtain heal-ing we are aligned with the truth of the divine plan, and all suffer-ing is resolved. At that point we move along in the direction of our divine plan.

Our beloved pets do not truly suffer, because they live in a state of awareness that is different from ours. That is, their minds don't get in-volved and judge experiences as good or bad—the root of our suffer-ing. Instead, our pets fully experience whatever moment they are in, with a very limited perspective of self-consciousness. This is certainly not to say they aren't self-aware—they fully are. They have the ability to make decisions derived from learned behavior. They have cognitive skills and intelligence. This is necessary for them to function in their day-to-day routines. Our pets are like young children before they ma-ture into adults. They are alive in the moment and in love with being.

Place a mirror in front of an infant, and you might witness an inquisitive moment. The infant will see an image of something that intrigues him, but he doesn't have the ability to understand that the image in the mirror is himself. A pet looking into the mirror will do the same thing. She will look at the image and pay it very little attention. Without self-awareness, there is no separation, no ego, and no story that the mind tells itself. And, without the busy mind telling a story, there is only awareness of being.

The Bible tells us, "Be still, and know that I am God" (Psalms 46:10). This means to attain stillness of the mind, and be aligned with an awareness of truth: that there is nothing that is separate; all things are of one being. Our pets have this stillness of mind.

We humans become so focused on the awareness of our busy minds that we have forgotten how to be aware of the stillness that directs us back toward truth. While we are listening to our mind telling us its favorite story, we narrow our focus to the point at which we tune out our state of being, and the story becomes the only truth. This is what separates us from our pets. They never lose that awareness of truth because they don't have a story that tells them otherwise—and because of this, they're naturally predisposed to a state of well-being. Even when illness occurs in our pets, there is always a healed state of being. Nothing, no story, no belief system, will move them away from that. They will never be *not* healed.

Denial and Truth

Our pets spend most of their time in an awareness aligned with truth, and without the storytelling mind, they live in an energetic state of love and compassion. This is why they love us unconditionally—they cannot love us any other way. They are in tune with their intuitive state of being, and a constant stream of intuitive energy flows in sync with their hearts. The result is a state of well-being, health, and harmony. In other words, as I said above, our pets are never *not* healed; they are in peak form for curing themselves, and they do not suffer, because there are no stories floating around in their little minds. Not a bad place to exist.

In contrast, imagine a person with cancer; he is angry that the doctors told him that he has cancer, and believes that he shouldn't have cancer. His mind races, telling him all the reasons why he shouldn't have cancer: *I won't live to see my grandchildren, I won't get to enjoy my retirement,* and so on. This causes great anguish. Not only does it cause mental suffering, but the negative energy inherent in this state of mind also puts great stress on the body, contributing to physical imbalance and disease.

Imagine now that this person is spending time with his dog or his child. He temporarily forgets the story that he has cancer and falls into the joy of being with his loving companion. At that moment, the cancer is still there, but his story is gone, and he is not suffering. This is not denial; it is the *truth.* At that moment, when his suffering has stopped and he is revealing his natural state of joy, he is healing himself. This might not be curing the cancer, but he's realigning himself with the truth of *not suffering.* During this time of joyful being, his suffering is gone, he's in harmony with his true self, and his body becomes a reflection of healing. Isn't this where we would prefer to be at times when we have imbalance and disease?

I once had a wonderful old dog named Cherie as a patient. Cherie had been diagnosed with terminal cancer. Her caretakers suffered greatly, struggling with all the stories they told themselves: *She must be suffering. She will soon die. We will never see her again. This shouldn't be happening.*

Let's look a little closer at these beliefs created by the mind.

— *She must be suffering.* Well, no, she can't suffer; she is incapable of suffering because she doesn't tell herself stories that cause suffering.

— *She will soon die.* This seems true, but is there really ever death? The body poops out, but the essence lives on, because it exists eternally. So, forget the suffering story of death, because it just isn't true.

— *We will never see her again.* Once Cherie's body is gone, can the caretakers no longer see their dog happy and living in harmony? Of course they can. All they have to do is shift their awareness and visualize in their minds the image of her being happy and healthy, and it is as real as it ever was.

— *This shouldn't be happening.* This is more suffering on the part of the caretakers, not the pet. They might never know why their dog has cancer. It's not important. What *is* important is relieving suffering, as that is the first step toward healing, and healing is living in a state of being, accepting that which comes, always joyful. *This* is where their dog is, even though someone told them a story about their wonderful dog having cancer.

This might seem like denial, but it is exactly the opposite. We don't deny that disease exists, and we don't ignore the possibility of doing something about it. But neither do we allow our minds to run off in a tizzy telling us all the reasons we should be suffering.

Because Cherie's caretakers had experienced so much suffering, I called in my animal-communicator friend, hoping she might shed some light that might give them comfort. Answering questions that I asked through the communicator, the lovely dog explained to us that her caretakers were drifting apart due to some personal problems in their home. When they became aware of the cancer in their dog, they reunited in the love for their pet. Cherie explained that it was part of her pathway to bring them back together.

Perhaps it was, perhaps not. It doesn't matter. What *does* matter is that the dog did not suffer and that she was in complete acceptance of her state of being.

The Energy Exchange

Imagine energy levels as a multistory house. Consider our normal energy balance to be the main floor, where we look around the house and outside the windows and see the yard and immediate neighbors. Now imagine that our energy level becomes heavy and contracted. This is like being down in the dark basement, where vision is impaired. If we don't remember what it is like in the main living area, then we will believe that our world is limited to only what we can perceive from the lower, basement level.

Now imagine we are upstairs at the highest level in the home: light and in harmony with our source energy. Our energy level is no longer weighed down by disturbing emotions, and we are aligned with truth; there is no suffering. From this perspective, we can see much farther, and our world appears different. We might look down the block and notice that our view is now much broader, and things are easier to understand. This is what it's like when we come from a higher energetic dimension, one of clarity. This is what our pet is experiencing, despite any illness.

When we expose our sick cat to the negative, dense energy we carry, it has a dramatic effect on the animal's overall energy balance. Our negative energy comingles with our cat's higher energy, and the push-pull of the two drags the cat down energetically to a level no longer conducive for the body to cure itself.

However, if we learn to control our reactive, emotionally charged stories and realign ourselves with our natural state of being, then we can infuse a positive energetic source into the cat's environment. The higher-level energy will comingle with the cat's energy and lift it to levels that promote the body's ability to function normally.

This is what our pets do *for us* when we are ill. They bring a positive source of energy that bolsters our own and helps us return to health and harmony. They do it without knowing, and that's precisely what *allows* them to do it. Sounds like a riddle, but it is the truth. The energetic exchange that occurs between us and our pets has been documented in the laboratory. As mentioned in Chapter Four, the research being done at the HeartMath Institute has paved the way to a scientific understanding of how this energetic exchange occurs, as well as its influence on our overall health. All we need to do is be aware that it is going on.

Once we become aware of the influence our minds have on our overall energetic states, we can find ways to help control and eliminate destructive emotions and thoughts that contribute to real physical imbalance and disease. At that point, we can have a direct impact on our healing and our ability to cure ourselves and those around us—namely, our pets.

With this foundational understanding, let's continue on to the next chapters and explore the essential, practical matters of holistically caring for your animal companion.

CHAPTER SIX

FINDING THE RIGHT VETERINARIAN

*"The art of healing comes from nature,
not from the physician. Therefore the physician
must start from nature, with an open mind."*

— PARACELSUS

If you've ever had to make an unexpected trip to the local animal emergency clinic, you understand the discomfort of meeting a new veterinarian in a stressful situation. Without the security of a familiar face, fears may arise that you wouldn't otherwise have experienced. Doubts could interfere when decisions need to be made. I spent three years as a veterinary clinician in an animal emergency hospital, witnessing fears and doubts that would not have existed if the caretakers and I had a previously established bond of trust.

Over the years, a bond will indeed most likely develop between you, your pet, and your veterinarian—which, as explained in Chapter Four, is an energetic connection. The trust and understanding the three of you share should increase with time and experience, and the strength of this bond will help you make decisions regarding your pet's health care throughout his or her life. Once it's been established, a sense of ease and confidence will flow through each veterinary visit. The importance of this bond, and the role it plays in the interactions between all parties, cannot be emphasized enough.

Most of us will have the opportunity to spend years with our beloved pets. We will share many experiences, highs and lows. Part of the honor of being pet caretakers is shouldering the responsibility of keeping our pets happy and healthy. Many times we'll need to seek guidance from professional health-care specialists, and it's critical that we take the time to select the right person for the job.

The Metamorphosis of the Veterinarian

Traditionally, veterinarians have been regarded with respect and seen to have a great deal of integrity, and they served an important role in the days when most people lived farm-based lives, prior to urbanization. This sentiment still exists today. Most veterinarians have a deep love and compassion for animals, apparent in their choice of veterinary medicine as a career. However, I have witnessed a change in my profession. The care and compassion are still evident, but an unfortunate barrier has developed that makes the crucial bond more difficult to establish. Let's take a closer look.

The image of the veterinarian has always been of the town's animal doctor donning a white coat, beaming a big smile, and holding a pet in his arms—evoking a feeling of comfort and a sense of confidence. The image was deserved and well represented by most veterinarians, who worked at mixed-animal practices and spent the day caring for farm animals as well as domestic pets. They came to our homes and farms day or night, sat at the kitchen table with us, and became an extension of our lives. Their compassion and dedication was respected by all.

Then a metamorphosis began.

Societal values shifted during the rebuilding after World War II. Technology began to make life easier, and the family structure gradually changed. People moved from their hometowns in search of better careers with bigger paychecks. As the economy prospered, we had more money with which to attain more numerous and better goods and services. We seemed to lose touch with the beauty and value of the simple things and the good, solid relationships within our communities. Life became faster paced as we ran to keep up with technology. Society demanded more from us, and we in turn demanded more from others. Relationships that once were simple now became more complicated, including our relationships with our pets. Though we still had deep connections with our animal companions, many of us bought into the assembly-line, impersonal style of health care for them. It was often cheaper and, we were told, better. One veterinarian was just as good as the next, as long as he or she followed the "scientific" protocol.

This metamorphosis in our thinking affected veterinary training. Future veterinarians still entered their careers with hearts filled with compassion, but training institutions began to focus on perfection of skills through scientific knowledge and technological advancements. The profession became very competitive; many fine individuals were turned away, unable to get into the field. Those who had been accepted into the veterinary colleges had similar personality profiles: Most of them fell into the type A category, with tremendous left-brain, analytical capabilities and a fiercely competitive drive for success.

During the four years of veterinary college, these aspiring veterinarians were inundated with factual, scientifically based research, intermingled with the latest technology. In clinical training, many were instructed to practice from a defensive perspective, assuming that every client who brought in a pet could (and would) sue them if they made a mistake. It shouldn't be surprising, then, that many of the young veterinarians coming out of school were walking textbooks, taught to practice from a fearful perspective.

Veterinarians became conditioned to work strictly with facts and showed little interest in the story surrounding those facts. As discussed in Chapter Two, this trend extends to our physicians as well. This new approach to health care narrowed the perspective of clinical medicine, and the whole was dissected down into individual parts. Each part now had a specialist who understood its form and function. Clinicians became focused on facts and details. Daniel H. Pink's book *A Whole New Mind* refers to a revealing study done at Stony Brook University Hospital in New York: The researchers found that in the examination room, when the patients began to narrate the history of their problems, within 23 seconds the doctor would interrupt and insist on hearing just the facts.

The left-brain emphasis on clinical medicine produced a computerlike approach to dealing with patients. In the exam room, data was obtained in the form of a detailed, specific history; a rundown of clinical symptoms; and a thorough examination. Then the clinician would make a preliminary list of different diagnoses and order ancillary testing that might include laboratory work, x-rays, and ultrasounds in order to confirm or rule out each potential diagnosis. Once a tentative diagnosis was made, a treatment protocol based on scientific evidence was started, with a predictable, probable outcome. At this point, the pet's caregiver would be told something like, "Your loved one has a tumor. We need to follow a chemotherapy plan, and the chances of success are slim."

I remember a phone call from a distressed former client who had moved to another town. Mira was obviously upset as she explained that Roxie, her middle-aged schnauzer, had been to see the new veterinarian for a lump on her skin. The veterinarian took a look and told Mira that the lump was probably cancerous and should be removed immediately. The lump was surgically removed and sent to the laboratory for analysis.

I tried to calm her down by telling her that we should consider some other possibilities. Roxie was still pretty young, and skin lumps were common for schnauzers. I explained that even though some were malignancies, most were benign. I also noted that if the lump turned out to be malignant, we could look into alternative modalities as another form of treatment—an approach that had seen a good deal of success.

Just spending a little time focusing on the bigger picture and showing empathy enabled Mira to calm her fears as she waited for the lab results. While I'm sure Roxie's new veterinarian was well-meaning, his emphasis on clinical results left no room for a spirit of trust or openness to possibility in the veterinarian-caretaker-pet relationship. What's more, several days later, Mira called again to let me know that the mass was a benign cyst, and the problem had been resolved.

Two Approaches, Two Different Assessments

It is certainly the responsibility of clinicians to focus on facts and details, but we can also expand our thoughts to include a broader range of possibilities and outcomes and, of course, the feelings of the people whose pets we are treating.

Let's use an example case scenario and compare the strictly left-brain, rational approach with what I like to call the "whole-brain" approach.

Rufus is a ten-year-old Rottweiler-mix dog who has been taken to the veterinary hospital because his human companion noticed that he is not acting like himself. The veterinarian walks into the examination room, where Rufus is standing near his companion. When approached, Rufus growls at the veterinarian.

"Hello, I'm Dr. Smith. What seems to be the problem with Rufus today?" asks the veterinarian.

"Hi, Dr. Smith, I'm Carla. Rufus hasn't been feeling well and doesn't want to eat his food. This has been going on for two days."

"Does Rufus usually have a good appetite?"

"Yes. He usually wolfs his food down."

"Has there been any vomiting or diarrhea?"

"He might have vomited once. I found some fluid on the carpet in the living room."

"What do you feed Rufus?"

"I feed him a premium lamb-and-rice dog food."

"Is there a chance that Rufus could have eaten anything to upset his stomach?"

"No, not that I know of, unless someone threw something in the backyard."

"Is he drinking water?"

"Yes, he seems to be drinking a bit more than usual."

"Have you noticed any weight loss?"

"No. He's always been a big fellow."

"That's fine. Is there anything else different that's going on with Rufus?"

"Let's see. Well, he growled at the kids if they got too close to him, but we figured that he was in pain and wanted to be left alone. He's on pain medication for his hips, you know. He has an odor coming from his ears. Also, he's been getting up every night at about one in the morning to go outside. But other than that, he's been pretty much the same."

Now, the left-brain approach will include the following as symptoms and history: listlessness, anorexia (off food) for 48 hours, vomiting of fluid once, polydipsia (drinking more water), ear odor, hip pain, and consumption of pain medication. This information leads to an initial analysis, which looks like the following list:

1. Vomiting and anorexia could be due to multiple internal diseases, including that of the kidney, liver, or pancreas, or a foreign body in the gastrointestinal tract.

2. Increased urination could be due to internal organ dysfunction, but diabetes and Cushing's disease also need to be considered as possibilities.

3. Odor from the ears usually means infection.

4. Hindquarter pain indicated by owner's report and prescribed medication is possibly due to dog's age and the presence of arthritis.

5. Nighttime trips to urinate are probably due to polydipsia.

If we look at the same findings and use the "facts," but expand our thinking to include the right-brain, holistic approach, then our initial assessment would be much the same—but would *also* include the following:

1. Anger is the emotional response when the liver is out of balance, and may be the cause of the growling.

2. Heat generation accompanies most liver imbalances and can cause ear infection.

3. Lamb-and-rice chow is a heat-generating diet.

4. The body's circadian clock highlights the liver between 1 A.M. and 3 A.M.—the organ is most active during this time—so getting up every night is possibly due to liver imbalance.

5. Liver imbalance can lead to pain and stiffness in the hindquarter joints and interfere with the normal downward flow of the gastrointestinal system, causing vomiting.

The next step is the examination. The veterinarian with a left-brain approach examines Rufus and finds an angry dog with infected ears who won't open his mouth, growls when his abdomen is touched, and sits down when his hindquarters are examined. The veterinarian detects some discomfort when putting slight pressure along the back. He gets a whiff of the dog's bad breath and takes note.

The veterinarian using a holistic approach identifies the same findings with Rufus but also recognizes that his black fur has auburn highlights and is dry and scruffy. Even though Rufus won't let the veterinarian look in his mouth, he is panting. The veterinarian sees that his tongue is dark red and thin and has a whitish-yellow coating on it. He also notices that his breath not only smells bad but has a distinctive foul and pungent quality. This veterinarian notes that the back pain is at the location of the liver alarm point, the tenth thoracic vertebrae.

The veterinarian with the left-brain approach has made a long list of potential problems and orders blood work, x-rays of the abdomen and the back, and a urinalysis with cortisol levels. He tells Rufus's human companion that her dog will probably need to be sedated to do the diagnostic testing.

The holistic veterinarian realizes that he can attribute all of Rufus's symptoms to a probable liver imbalance. He knows that the liver is greatly affected by sedation and tries to avoid going this route unless absolutely needed. The veterinarian tells Rufus's caretaker that he would like to give Rufus a Bach Flower Remedy, a natural calming tonic that will not affect the liver, an hour before any further diagnostic testing is to be done. The Bach remedy will calm him enough so that the testing can be performed without sedation. The veterinarian focuses first on the liver as the cause of the problems, thus eliminating any unneeded, and expensive, ancillary diagnostic testing.

Empathy and the Clinician's Intention

In *A Whole New Mind,* Daniel H. Pink also refers to a study that reveals how empathy (a right-brain function) diminishes with each year that a student spends in medical school. Empathy is the ability to put oneself in another person's situation and intuitively feel what he or she feels. Essentially, it is feeling *with* someone. If a clinician's right-brain function has reduced his capacity to have empathy for his patients, then those intuitively guided abilities will be limited. Pink explains that the "detached scientific model" of the left-brain approach "is appropriate but insufficient."

When clinicians have empathy for patients, they become attuned with the patients' energy. Once this happens, guidance may come from a deeper intuitive level that cannot yet be explained by the scientific model. Alternative considerations and unconventional ideas, formed from holistically examining a patient, may lead the clinician to explore possibilities that would have otherwise been overlooked.

Over the years, I've found that the most important information a veterinarian can possess is the awareness of his or her own intention. I've gone so far as to place notes in strategic places in my clinics to remind the veterinarians and staff to remember their intention when working with a sick or injured pet.

It is imperative that *you* understand each veterinarian's intention when deciding who will care for your pet. Intention sets in motion powerful energies that initiate action and direct results. The law of cause and effect, which has also been referred to as "What you sow, so shall you reap," plays a large role in how we heal ourselves and our pets. A principle based on cause and effect states that when we create a thought and combine it with an emotion, if the thought and emotion persist, a universal energy source will respond in accordance with that thought. *We can effect change through our thoughts and emotions!* The thoughts that set this process in motion are driven by our intentions, which become a powerful source for initiating healing and directing the outcome.

Let's look at a hypothetical situation: You come home from a late evening at work. You find that your pet has vomited all over the carpet and obviously feels awful. Your mind responds to the situation and tells you that there is a problem. It reasons that the pet is probably ill and you need to act. Now you initiate your intention. You tell yourself, *I am going to do something to help my pet.* This thought is driven by your emotions of compassion, caring, and love, and becomes a powerful energy mover. The universe is activated. Your mind concludes that you should drive your pet to the veterinary hospital as soon as possible. You take action, grab your pet, and head out the door.

When you arrive at the veterinary hospital, it becomes obvious that they are preparing to close for the evening. You are welcomed into the hospital and taken immediately to the exam room.

Hypothetical Veterinarian A is told that there is a sick pet waiting in the exam room. He remembers that his child has a basketball game that evening and realizes that examining and treating the pet will most likely cause him to be late to the game. The veterinarian is a very compassionate and caring individual, but his mind becomes distracted by the time factor. Unknowingly, he's shifted his intention from helping the pet to resolving the problem in a timely manner so he'll make it to the game on time. When he enters the exam room, his intention is generating energy to resolve both the pet's problem and the time issue, while *your* intention is generating energy simply to resolve your pet's health problem. Because these intentions are opposed, the energy that moves and directs healing has been diminished.

Hypothetical Veterinarian B is told that you are with your pet in the exam room. She's aware that her child has a basketball game and that she might be late to his game. However, she stays focused on her intention to help resolve your pet's health problem. She enters the room with her intention generating energy for your pet's healing. This harmonious energy, derived from two people with the same intention, has a very powerful effect on moving the universal energy toward the intended outcome. This is the very premise at the base of group prayer: a group of people pray with the same intention (energy plus emotion), knowing that the synchronicity of the energy produced by the group will be a potent method for directing a specific result.

If we look even closer at intention, we uncover the most powerful source of initiating healing that we as humans can provide. Years ago, I had just begun expanding my practice to embrace a more holistic approach and incorporating alternative modalities. I was attending a national veterinary conference that included several lectures about using alternative or complementary treatments with pet medicine. One of the speakers was a renowned alternative veterinary practitioner whom I was eager to hear. I sat in amazement throughout her discussion and felt very fortunate to witness her presentation.

As luck would have it, after the lunch break, I was sitting on a bench outside the lecture room when the speaker walked over and sat by me. We exchanged greetings, and I told her how much I enjoyed her presentation. We continued to talk, and I began to realize that she had many of the same feelings I had about pet healing. I was usually reluctant to share my thoughts about healing from a nonscientific perspective, but I felt comfortable doing so with her.

As our discussion progressed, I found myself asking, "With the many alternative approaches to healing that are now offered, how do you choose which one will be most beneficial for the pet?"

She smiled and answered, "One day you will know what healing is all about. Then it won't make any difference if you choose needles, herbs, or whatever. You will have realized that it is all about your intention."

At the time, her statement was a compelling and mysterious revelation. Today, I am at that place of understanding, and I'm forever indebted to her for planting that seed in my mind. Now, I hope to pass this revelation on to you.

When we begin to understand the importance of intention in directing action and results, particularly in regard to healing, we can accept the empowerment that comes with this knowledge. Whether we make the treatment decisions as veterinarians or as pet caretakers, our intentions ultimately direct the course of healing and the outcome. Scientific knowledge and experience are certainly necessary to inform decisions when veterinarians are recommending treatment. However, if their intentions are focused solely on the pet's *healing*—and they are open to guidance—then those decisions may be aided by insights that result from empathy and originate from a deeper source of healing power than medical diagnosis can provide.

Determining Intention

It's sometimes hard to identify another person's intention, but if you look for subtle hints, it usually reveals itself. Though anyone—including a veterinarian—can have an off day occasionally, character traits displayed consistently over time will often illuminate an individual's intention. Moreover, if you can attune with the veterinarian's energy, you'll feel whether you are aligned with similar energies. (When dissimilar energies come in contact, we often have a feeling of wanting to *get away*.) Pay attention to the feelings that arise when you're with your veterinarian. Your feelings will not mislead you even though you might try to rationalize them away.

Your pet can be a great indicator to you of another person's intentions. Because pets live totally in the moment, they're also masters of reading the situation at hand. Feelings like love and compassion create light and soothing vibrational energies, whereas fearful feelings vibrate at much lower frequencies, causing discomfort and agitation. The energies might be coming from conscious or unconscious beliefs on the part of the veterinarian, but to pets, they are very real and very telling. If pets feel comfortable with the energetic connection between them and the veterinarian, they will let you know by showing signs of acceptance.

Of course, there are those pets with fearful personalities (more on that in Chapter Eight) or that have had bad experiences that might provoke fearful responses. In these cases, the caretaker will have to rely on knowledge of the pet to determine whether the fear is due to the veterinarian or is a typical response to unfamiliar people and situations.

I'm embarrassed to admit that there are veterinarians who spend a lot of time focusing on the bottom line. But of course, veterinarians are human beings, and we are all subject to a variety of concerns. That said, if a veterinarian becomes overly focused on monetary gain, there might be a shift of intention; helping the pet might become secondary to financial motives. If we accept the intention principle and its influence on healing, we realize that if the intention is on the financial situation (whether consciously or unconsciously), the results of the healing process could be altered.

It can be difficult to determine whether finances are involved in a veterinarian's intentions, but there are subtle signs you can look for. For example, these veterinarians can become defensive when asked to explain charges. Concerns about being compensated create energy that vibrates at a lower level than do love and compassion. While this is not necessarily negative energy, it's less conducive to healing than higher-level energy.

Also be aware of situations that make you feel physically bad inside (usually in the gut area). Again, certain intentions generate lower-level energy frequencies and are easy to detect if you become aware of your own feelings. Trust your instincts, and if you feel unsettled, or feel any reservations, consider finding another veterinarian who resonates with you and your pet.

The Ego in Medicine

Another quality I like to see in a veterinarian is a humble attitude while working with pets and their caregivers. A lot of veterinarians, like most scientific, left-brain–dominated clinicians, are skilled at overcoming difficult and challenging situations by eliminating fears that often delay necessary action. These individuals can "take the bull by the horns" and assume control using accurate and detailed deductive reasoning, often leading to outstanding results delivered in a timely manner.

However, when this skill becomes a dominating factor and ego is involved, there is a tendency to overlook the fact that we are all humans with human limitations. There are many times that we clinicians need to acknowledge that we might not have all the answers for a sick pet. Humility allows us to step back and ask ourselves, *What have I missed?* It allows us to seek help, call another veterinarian for a consultation, or admit when we can't find the answer. The humble veterinarian understands that it is perfectly normal to admit that he or she does not have a solution to every problem. The veterinarian remains focused on the intention to direct healing and removes the ego from the equation.

Research has proven that the ego is a product of the activity of the brain's left hemisphere. Rational inference and deductive reasoning are two of the left hemisphere's main functions. The ego is very important in all aspects of life because it helps us with decision making, usually from a protective or defensive perspective. The ego develops when we realize that we are separate beings from our parents and that there are elements in the world that might either help us or harm us. The ego teaches us not to step out in front of the bus or otherwise put ourselves in harm's way. It also gives us the drive to take on arduous tasks and push ourselves.

When clinicians are trained and continually immersed in strictly left-brain thought processes, the ego has a tendency to dominate our creative problem solving that might help in our conclusions. I call this "getting in the way of ourselves." The ego will not allow those intuitively guided thoughts to appear in our consciousness, because these thoughts will not usually be aligned with deductive reasoning.

But the problem with such a "just the facts" approach to health and healing lies in its limitations. Many times we clinicians run the gamut of left-brain deductive reasoning and take a rational approach to solving the problem at hand, only to find out that it doesn't work. Most likely we will rack our brains trying to figure out where we went wrong or what we missed. Ultimately, we become frustrated and give up. Then we either present the situation to the pet's caretaker as incurable or recommend a specialist who might have further training that will help reveal the answer.

It is in these times that we need to remove the ego from the picture and move into the right-brain realm for guidance. Veterinarians who open their minds to a more holistic perspective of pet health care will naturally expand their abilities to encompass a balanced, whole-brain approach that aligns with natural healing. When a veterinarian accepts the possibility that alternative modalities can have positive results *without* scientific explanation, the blinders are removed. The ego subsides, and in moves an intuitive guidance source that's both potent and dependable. Rational thought combined with intuition is the most powerful tool set we have as clinicians, and it will guide us to take correct action to direct healing.

For example, I recently did corrective knee surgery for a dog's ruptured ligament, a procedure I'd done hundreds of times over the years without complication. However, this dog developed continual pain when placing weight on the leg. I did a thorough examination of the affected leg and found no obvious reason for the pain. My left-brain thinking began its immediate deductive reasoning. It told me, *Let's see, the pain could be due to this or that . . .* So, I would check these options out.

After examining these possibilities and not finding an answer, my ego kicked in and asked me, *Hey, did you overlook something in surgery that could have caused this?* I immediately began to sweat and look for an answer that would cast the light on another solution. I told myself, *I've done this procedure hundreds and hundreds of times, and this has never happened.* You can imagine the frustration setting in. You can also imagine the subtle shift of intention away from directing healing to one of self-defense.

I decided to step back and start over, thinking that I could still rationally resolve the problem. I scheduled the pet to return the next day for a barrage of tests and x-rays that would hopefully help diagnose the issue at hand.

That night in bed I found myself going over all the possibilities of things I could have overlooked, until I became mentally and emotionally fatigued. Then I let my guard down, and a little voice from inside said, *Hey, you know how this works. Turn this over to a higher source.*

I smiled and nodded, and I said out loud, "I'm having a little trouble with this, and I need some help solving this problem." I felt at ease knowing that I would get the help I needed, and turned over and went to sleep.

The next morning I had forgotten my request for help as I went through my morning routine of preparing for the day. While shampooing my hair in the shower, a thought popped into my head: *The pet's problem is a mild infection between the joint capsule and the skin.* Then it continued by saying, *Oh, yeah. That cat you treated last week actually had another issue . . .* and gave me the answer to that problem as well.

I knew beyond a shadow of a doubt that this was not my imagination but some intuitive guidance that had been given to me from a deeper, all-knowing source of information. After my shower, I notified my secretary to phone the dog's caretaker, cancel the further testing, and have him come in for medication that would resolve the infection. Two days later, the caretaker called to let us know that his pet was back to normal.

A Director of Healing

Don't be afraid to communicate your desire for holistic care for your pets. Change happens slowly, but if more people demand holistic practices from their veterinarians, it will come. The expression "Seeing is believing" holds true in many situations. Even those who are used to operating within the strictly rational approach can change their minds when presented with irrefutable evidence. When veterinarians start to accept that alternative modalities and complementary treatments for pets might be beneficial, they will become more open-minded about the possibility that different philosophies on healing have some validity.

Recall the story in Chapter Two about the debilitated horse treated with acupuncture. I remember asking myself why we had not previously been told about this amazing form of treatment. Here was this horse that, after having been given all our Western medical treatment options without any notable improvement in his terrible back pain, was now acting clinically normal. This was a great opportunity for each of us to open our minds to the possibility that alternative treatment modalities might have some value. Fortunately, a couple of the clinicians at the veterinary school hospital were intrigued and learned to use acupuncture in the treatment of animals. Within a short period of time, those clinicians went on to resolve several conditions in the horse that previously had been accepted as untreatable.

Holistic veterinarians understand the importance of rationality and deductive Western medicine and its tremendous benefits for pets—but they have also accepted its limitations. Their expanded mind-set removes expectations and looks toward the unexplainable. They become aware that they're not healers but *directors* of healing, enabling patients' bodies to restore themselves once they've helped remove the obstacles to well-being.

With this new awareness, holistic veterinarians can start to move away from the story that tells them they alone are in charge of living and dying, of healing and health—and instead occupy a new role in the interaction between the pet and the caretaker. The role might be the wise voice of experience when making decisions, the teacher of new methods of pet care, or the compassionate, consoling friend during a grieving period. When we veterinarians become aware of the multiple roles we occupy, we can focus on doing the best job we can, while removing all preconceived notions that might limit the outcome.

Choosing a veterinarian is as difficult as choosing your family physician. Make the effort to do a little digging; find out if your candidates are using complementary modalities. What are their reputations in the community? Spend some time during your first visit discussing philosophies about pet care. Be open about your expectations, and try to get a sense of what their intentions are with regard to your pet. Voice your desire to include complementary healing methods and take a holistic approach to pet health care.

Choosing a veterinarian is not like choosing a mechanic. Sure, you want someone who has experience, is honest, and does a good job, but more important, you want someone whose deeper beliefs and intentions are aligned with yours. That doesn't matter when restoring a car to operational status, but I hope by now it's crystal clear why it matters immensely when restoring your pet's body to well-being.

CHAPTER SEVEN

BALANCING YOUR PET'S BODY

"Let food be thy medicine, and medicine be thy food."

— HIPPOCRATES

Well-being is our natural state. It comes from pure, unadulterated source energy that provides us and our pets with healthy, joyful lives. Maintaining this natural state in the physical dimension requires that we stay balanced at *each* dimensional level. We can have an infection in the physical dimension and cure this disorder with the use of drugs. If, at the same time, though, we are an emotional wreck, then we are not balanced, and we are not healthy.

As we've already discussed, the physical body is made up of the energetic body, and many, many things affect it both positively and negatively. Some of these we're incapable of detecting. Many times it is difficult, if not impossible, to find the source of our imbalance or our pet's, which is where a trusted holistic clinician comes in. However, we can get a great head start establishing general well-being in the first place by promoting good foundational health.

This chapter will provide insight into caring for your pet's body, centering on nutrition, since so much of what we commonly think of as pet care revolves around the diet you feed your pet. And the following chapter, Chapter Eight, on mind and spirit, will expand this perspective beyond the physical dimension and explore the mental and spiritual aspects of well-being.

The Nutrition to Thrive

Many books have been written about nutrition, providing a framework of guidelines regarding balanced nutrition for each species and giving advice according to the latest in scientific research. Over the past 50 years, we've learned a great deal about human nutrition—or more to the point, what diseases improper nutrition can cause. This is very much the case for pet nutrition as well. However, if we are to provide a healthy, balanced lifestyle for our pets, we have to go far *beyond* what the latest nutritional research tells us.

Research dictates the importance of nutritional requirements, including protein, carbohydrates, vitamins, minerals, and much more. Deficiencies or imbalances in these requirements may lead to certain diseases. But research also captures just a *portion* of the role nutrition plays in promoting a healthy, balanced life. It would be like scientifically analyzing a brick in the hope that it would explain how to build a house. Certainly there is much more to a house, as a whole, than the physical components of the brick.

To find a holistic approach that will help us provide harmony in body, mind, and spirit for our pets, let's begin by expanding our perspective on nutrition.

An Individual Approach to Nutrition

Historically, nutritional guidelines derived from scientific research have been based on general populations and disregard the requirements of the individual. We are led to believe that there can be scientifically formulated pet food that will be beneficial for all. This approach assumes that, because we've identified the nutritional components required for a particular species, a diet that fulfills those requirements will be in *each* individual pet's best interest.

This is far from the truth.

In the United States, the thinking on pet nutrition has paralleled the more generalized perspective regarding basic health—a one-size-fits-all perspective. In the early years, commercial pet foods were produced for an entire species—for dogs, cats, horses, and so on. In time, as pet-nutrition research advanced, the focus narrowed a bit, with different diets for puppies and kittens. When the market for the standard diets became saturated, companies started looking for new markets, leading them to research diets for senior pets, giant breeds, small breeds, and countless others. Specialty diets for pets with specific diseases became popular with veterinarians, and that market thrived. However, to date, the commercial pet-food industry and pet-nutrition research has failed to recognize the importance of a diet structured for the *individual* pet's needs.

When we select a diet for our pet, if it does not meet the individual's needs, then despite the fact that it fulfills the general requirements for that species, our pet will suffer imbalances that will eventually lead to physical disease.

At that time, it is the veterinarian's responsibility to recognize the diet's role in creating the imbalances that led to the disease. Unfortunately, most veterinarians in the United States have been trained with the same scientific principles that are used in nutritional research for pets.

However, in many other parts of the world, the importance of individual nutritional requirements has long been recognized. For thousands of years, in China and other countries of the East, the qualities and needs of the individual are defined by his or her *constitution*. In Traditional Chinese Medicine, each individual falls into one of five element categories. Through identifying an individual's element, or constitution, nutritional guidelines can be applied to maintain the harmony and balance of that individual.

Similarly, Ayurvedic medicine has been practiced in India for 3,000 years and is still one of the predominant forms of medicine used today in that country. The Ayurvedic perspective states that the main cause of disease is improper nutrition, and balancing the diet is the primary tool for maintaining health and treating disease. Much like

Traditional Chinese Medicine, this philosophy begins by recognizing the importance of individual needs. Ayurveda identifies three primary patterns of energy (that also govern metabolism), referred to as *doshas.* Ayurvedic practitioners believe that each individual consists of all three doshas, but that one dosha is dominant over the other two, and its dominance affects the character of the individual.

Specifics of both these modalities—Traditional Chinese Medicine and Ayurvedic medicine—will be covered in depth in Chapter Nine, but for now it suffices to say that when I refer to "individual needs," I'm essentially referring to the primary difference that separates traditional medicine, such as TCM and Ayurveda, from Western medicine, which tends to overgeneralize and be limited in its approach. A holistic veterinarian can help assess a pet's individual needs based on a combination of factors (age, sex, environment, constitution, and so on). And nutrition is a key component of that.

So, it's critical that we identify the dietary and nutritional needs of the individual pet and focus on a holistic, preventive program. With that said, one factor in any healthy, balanced diet would be ensuring that we use high-quality ingredients. Let's take a look at the pet-food industry and see how it stacks up.

The Evolution of the Pet-Food Industry

For generations, people fed leftover table scraps to their pets as their primary diet. Then in the middle of the last century, the concept of "pet food" emerged as an answer to two aims: (1) to produce a new national market, and (2) to find a way to utilize scraps and by-products from the human food industry that, until then, had been disposed of. So, manufacturers began producing a pet food—filled with grains, cheap carbohydrates (like corn), and meat scraps considered unfit for human consumption. The marketing strategy emphasized ease and inexpensiveness for the pet owner. Nothing in the manufacturers' intent had anything to do with providing a nutritionally sound diet for the animal.

Pet-food marketing used high-profile celebrities to promote products. I remember watching television commercials in the old days with Lorne Green (who played the character Ben Cartwright on the television series *Bonanza*) sitting in a chair petting his Irish setter, telling us he fed his dogs Alpo because Alpo consisted only of meat and meat by-products. If it was good enough for old Ben Cartwright's dog, then it surely would be good enough for ours. No one would dare question the integrity of Mr. Cartwright, much less look at the content of the diet.

The next stage in commercial pet-food development came with the technology to produce a dry, or "kibble," form. The consumer could simply open a bag, scoop a cup of dry pet food, and place it in a bowl. No-hassle feeding. Commercial pet-food companies again provided the consumer with a diet based on convenience, instead of nutritional quality. We really can't blame people for selecting their pets' food in this manner in the past. It was essentially all we had to offer our pets.

Then, however, something happened that changed the industry: A major company began to make foods designed for pets with specific illnesses. The company researched the specific nutritional needs of those with diseases such as kidney insufficiency, intestinal disorders, diabetes, urinary disease, and many more. Over a short period of time, implementing these diets in diseased pets showed remarkable results. It became standard veterinary practice to incorporate these special diets into routine protocols for treating pets with these diseases. The pet foods were sold by veterinarians only.

These diets were far from ideal, but their development was crucial in the evolution of the pet-food industry, because the *intention* of a section of the industry changed. Instead of focusing on disposing unwanted by-products and improving bottom-line profits, the new intention included a shift toward concentrating on the nutritional needs of the pet.

Several years later, the same company decided to expand their market to include commercial diets for pets without diseases (supposedly healthy pets). The new focus created the need for research that led to the development of nutritionally balanced food for both dogs and cats. In my many years of clinical practice in veterinary medicine, I had never witnessed such an impact on overall pet health care as I did when these new pet foods were introduced. In no time, most of the pets on these diets were much healthier. Older dogs that had been placed on the "senior" diet were more active and youthful. Common gastrointestinal upsets were reduced. Caretakers everywhere raved about how much healthier and happier their pets became.

Not only were the results surprising to pet owners, but they were also an eye-opener for the veterinary community. Veterinarians began to recognize the benefits of feeding animals a nutritionally balanced diet, despite a historic, community-wide apathetic attitude toward this topic. Indeed, learning about nutrition just doesn't seem to inspire most veterinarians. I would venture that if we peeked into a nutrition class at any veterinary college today, we would find most of the students fighting to keep awake.

Most clinicians are problem solvers by nature—it's part of what attracts us to medicine. And we like to solve problems quickly. But the results of a wholesome, balanced diet are *not* immediate. Nutrition takes time; it is about building a foundation and watching for long-term effects. Veterinarians have a hard time concentrating on nutrition as part of their problem-solving tool kit, because they can't say, "Go home, change your pet's diet, and call me tomorrow to tell me how it works."

To be clear, veterinarians know that nutrition is important, but it's not considered a critical factor in why your pet may or may not be in optimal health. So as a community, most veterinarians don't tend to pay much attention to it. This is why asking many veterinary hospitals what diets they recommend will give you a plethora of answers.

As time went by and pets continued to show signs of improved health while on balanced diets, the pet-food market share began to shift. The companies that had thrived for years with their nutritionally unbalanced formulas started to feel the profit pinch as more pet owners opted to pay the higher prices for a more beneficial product. In a short period, some of the established companies began to manufacture recipes derived from the same health-conscious perspective, which were distributed to both veterinarians and pet-food stores. The pet-food giants that had profited for years from manufacturing poor-quality products still continued to do so, selling them through grocery stores.

We were now witnessing the development of two standards for pet foods: (1) the high-quality, high-cost diets that were nutritionally better for the pet and sold at the veterinary hospital or pet store; and (2) the lesser-quality, low-cost diet that might not be nutritionally balanced and was sold at the grocery store.

The new diets were still not perfect, because they were produced using less-than-ideal methods, such as heat-processing dry kibble, which essentially strips food of its natural nutrients. Still, their emergence forced the pet-food industry to refocus its intent toward producing a much healthier diet. The industry expanded, and as new companies joined the market, it became very competitive.

Americans began to focus on health consciousness for themselves and their pets alike; this created an even newer target market of those wanting a pet food that was nutritious and balanced, as well as made of wholesome ingredients. The gap between the quality of diet available to the human and to the pet began to narrow, to the delight of many pet caretakers. Custom diets appeared, featuring high-quality nutrients for pets of all ages and specific needs, which further aligned the quality of pets' and their caretakers' diets.

This had an enormous impact on pets' overall health: Life expectancy increased, and quality of life improved. We veterinarians love to take the credit for the increased longevity, with our new medications and technology; however, in my opinion, the availability of better-quality commercial pet food was primarily responsible for the change.

Demystifying Diets

Today, the commercial pet-food industry has provided many options, each claiming to be the best diet available. Walk into any large pet store and take a look: Diets come in moist (canned), semi-moist, and dry forms, with labels featuring an entire range of health-conscious buzzwords like *natural, holistic, hypoallergenic,* and *organic.* No wonder the caretaker rushes to the vet's office in a state of complete confusion! Unfortunately, most veterinarians know little more than the consumer about what is on the shelves and which diets are truly in the best interest of the pet. Veterinarians will be happy to share their experience and advice, but question them on the specifics of a particular diet and, more often than not, you'll find that they will be just as in the dark as you are.

The fact is, *there is no diet that will meet the nutritional requirements of all pets within a species.* Despite the best efforts of the pet-food industry to convince you otherwise, pets are individuals and should be fed accordingly. That said, let's start by looking at the basic requirements for our pets and then expand on that information.

The first thing we need to know is that cats and dogs are carnivores, not omnivores. This means that their entire biological system is based on the utilization of meat. Anything that deviates from this foundation will move the pet toward imbalance and will eventually lead to physical disease. Please remember the following: *Dogs and cats will not benefit from high-carbohydrate diets. Period.* Even though we have domesticated our dogs and cats over the many years we have coexisted, their physiological function has not changed. They are still meat eaters, and the closer their diet resembles their prey in the wild, the better for their health.

A leading veterinary nutritionist once remarked that the best diet for a cat would be a bag of mice. Obviously, that won't be on sale at your local grocery store anytime soon, but there are ways we can get close enough to natural food choices to provide our animal companions with balanced, wholesome diets.

Even though we know that dogs and cats are carnivores that would benefit from a high-protein diet, we continue to find large percentages of carbohydrates in most commercial pet foods. The reason here is financial. It costs a whole lot more to fill a food bag with animal protein than with a carbohydrate, like corn or rice. The pet-food industry is still trying to convince caretakers that carbohydrates are healthy for pets. While it is true that our pets may *survive* on diets high in carbohydrates, it in no way means that this type of diet is in their best interest. For pets to *thrive* and maintain balance, they must be fed a diet that meets their essential physiological needs.

Omnivores, like humans, eat both meat and plants. Their digestive systems are structured so that carbohydrates can be used as a rapid source of energy. Therefore, the human digestive system will utilize carbohydrates in an efficient manner without harm to the human, if balanced with protein, fat, minerals, and vitamins. Carnivores, on the other hand, have completely different digestive and metabolic systems. They don't have the ability to efficiently utilize carbohydrates; adding them to their diet creates an imbalance that leads to metabolic disturbances and physical disease.

Dogs and cats utilize protein and fat as their energy source and have no need for carbohydrates, such as corn, rice, wheat, and potatoes, which are converted and stored in the body as fat. Obesity, caused by overfeeding carbohydrates, has been linked to diabetes, arthritis, pancreatitis, and liver disease. I suspect that there are links to many more diseases that medical science has not yet proven. We now know that the protein-to-carbohydrate ratio in the cat and dog diet is tremendously important and should be one of the primary considerations when making food selections.

In fact, the carbohydrates that are in many commercial pet foods affect our dogs and cats in different adverse ways. Carbohydrates can either be *simple* or *complex,* depending on their chemical makeup. (The simpler in structure, the easier and quicker the carb can be utilized by the omnivore—not the carnivore.)

- **Simple carbohydrates,** or the sugars found in corn, rice, and wheat, are commonly used in commercial pet foods. These carbohydrates may lead to inappropriate blood-sugar-level fluctuations and predispose dogs and cats to obesity and related diseases.

- **Complex carbohydrates** are found in potatoes, beans, veggies, and fruit. They are difficult for dogs and cats to digest, and this may lead to digestive upset.

Many years ago, a leading veterinary nutritionist was studying a group of diabetic cats. Each had been diagnosed with insulin-dependent diabetes, which was only controlled with twice-a-day insulin injections. The nutritionist believed that the carbohydrates in these cats' diets were the predisposing factor for the diabetes, and she placed them on a moist, high-protein, low-carbohydrate diet. As she suspected, a more "natural" diet—one that coincided with what they would be eating in the wild and that was based on protein instead of carbohydrates—reestablished metabolic balance and eliminated the diabetes. *Each of the diabetic cats was successfully taken off the insulin.*

Research may tell us that dogs and cats do not need carbohydrates in their diet, yet even the most "natural" pet food still contains them because of the way it is processed. Dry pet food requires that a certain amount of carbohydrate be added to the kibble to "stick" the food together. This is why canned foods often have a higher ratio of protein to carbohydrate than dry food. However, pet-food manufacturers that have eliminated simple sugars and have opted for veggies and fruit as their carbohydrate have produced a much higher-quality kibble with less potential for causing imbalance and disease.

Form vs. Function: Dry, Canned, and Raw Options

Let's switch gears a bit to discuss the forms of commercial pet food, and gain more insight into what, exactly, we're putting into our pets' food bowls:

— As I mentioned earlier, when pet-food companies developed **dry** pet food, or kibble, they provided caretakers with the ultimate convenient food form. One quick scoop into the bag and *voilà!* The meal is ready. The intention was to create a product that was easy to prepare and store, at a price the market would bear. The intention was *not* about producing a diet that was wholesome and complete. Unfortunately, the pet-food industry wasn't willing to give the consumer the option.

Processing dry pet food has, since its inception, required two basic elements: heat and pressure. In order to deliver the final dry kibble, a wet form of the food is exposed to extreme heat and pressure. As the external structure of the food is altered, so is the internal structure, and some nutrients are lost. Yet in order for the food to meet minimum government requirements, it must contain certain nutrients. If those natural nutrients are lost in the processing, the company is forced to replace them by *inserting* a chemical substitution. Then the food is altered again as most producers add preservatives to increase shelf life and additives to enhance the flavor and appearance. By the time the dry kibble is in its final form, it no longer resembles the original food nutritionally. *The nutrient profile has changed dramatically.*

— **Canned** and **semi-moist** forms of pet food are not altered as much as the dry kibble, but they, too, are processed with additives and preservatives and do not have the nutritional value that pets need to thrive.

— Recently, several custom pet-food companies have begun offering pet meals that are prepared in their natural form, then **freeze-dried,** and packaged. The food is shipped frozen; the caretaker may prepare it by thawing it and feeding it to their pet raw or cooking it. This can be a very good option if the caretaker will take the time to find out the pet's individual nutritional needs and locate the appropriate diet, or have it custom-made. A holistic veterinarian can help determine the individual pet's requirements.

— This brings us to **raw** diets. The intention with a raw diet is to consume food that has had minimal alteration of its nutritional content, which typically occurs in processing or cooking. The hope is that eating raw foods will provide the maximal nutritional benefit available from the food source. A balanced, raw diet most closely resembles what our animals would be eating if they were still living in the wild. I believe that this is a good intention, and I have seen many pets thrive on raw diets. I also tell my clients that each pet must be addressed individually and that all factors must be considered before introducing a raw-food diet.

Regarding the raw diet particularly, we must take a number of factors into consideration. Allow me to briefly bring up one tenet of Traditional Chinese Medicine. (I will cover this philosophy in depth in Chapter Nine.) As many pets move into their senior years, their internal thermometers—their balance of heat and cold—often shift. According to TCM, the internal flame is beginning to flicker, and the body temperature starts to cool. The result of this shift in core body temperature will cause the pet to seek out warmth. This is why we often see older dogs or cats curled up in front of the warm fire or lying in the patch of sunlight coming through a window. It's critical that we offer these senior pets a diet that is *warming* in nature to offset the cold imbalance. We can do this by warming the food before feeding and selecting ingredients that will best produce internal heat (see list, below). We need to be aware of the body-temperature changes as our pets age; a raw, cold diet is probably not in the best interest of older pets.

Your veterinarian should be able to identify your pet's constitution and give you sound advice on whether a raw diet would be optimal for your animal companion. Determining your pet's constitution will let you know if he or she has a tendency to produce too much internal heat, *or* if he or she is prone to cool body temperatures and often seeks out heat. Those pets that fall into the latter category will benefit from ingredients that provide internal warmth and should avoid diets that cool.

Here's a short list with examples of both warming and cooling foods.

Warming foods:	Cooling foods:
Chicken	Turkey
Beef	Pork
Lamb	Rabbit
Venison	Cod
White rice	Brown rice
Oats	Millet
Asparagus	Barley
Onion	Spinach
Carrots	Kelp
Potato	Celery
Pumpkin	
Squash	

Transitioning Your Pet's Diet

I am asked time and time again what type of diet I recommend for pets. My standard answer is that, in order for them to thrive instead of just survive, they need a diet that is individually balanced and made from wholesome ingredients. The closer to the diet the animal would eat in its natural environment, the better.

Feeding your pet processed, commercial food will *not* meet these requirements. A wholesome, balanced meal—prepared and frozen by a commercial pet-food company or at home by you—will give your pet its best opportunity to thrive. If your pet can be fed raw, that would be optimal.

Many times people tell me that they decided to make the switch to a wholesome, fresh diet, but when they introduced it, their pets developed diarrhea. They took their animals to their regular veterinarian and were told that they couldn't handle the diet—it was too "rich." Chances are that the transition from processed food to a wholesome diet was made too quickly, and the intestines reacted to the change. Most pets have been fed processed diets for many years. The intestinal wall is no longer healthy, so the intestines are incapable of handling the wholesome diet.

The transition from a processed diet, particularly a dry kibble, must happen slowly over several weeks. If your pet has a history of stomach upset or intestinal disease, the transition may take months. However, we must remember that in order to heal the intestinal wall, it is imperative that we remove from the diet the food responsible for the damage. The time and commitment are well worth the effort.

To make a slow transition from processed to fresh pet food, calculate the amount of the current processed food fed to the pet over 24 hours. Then divide that amount into three feedings.

1. The first two feedings should use the current processed food, and the last feeding should introduce the new balanced, wholesome food. This should be done for two weeks while watching for digestive issues, such as vomiting, diarrhea, or loss of appetite.

2. If all is well after two weeks, then change the second feeding of processed food to the wholesome diet. Again, watch for digestive upset.

3. If all is well after another two weeks, then the remaining feeding of processed food can be changed to the fresh food, and the pet can be kept on the fresh, wholesome diet.

If your pet has difficulty adjusting, a holistic veterinarian can recommend supplements that will help the intestines heal during the transition. In a short period of time, you'll notice improvements in your pet's health, and there's a good chance you will enhance the quality of life, and extend the lifespan, of your beloved pet.

Research has shown that dry, processed kibble causes inflammation of the intestinal walls. This is often referred to as *leaky gut syndrome.* When the intestinal wall is damaged by diet, it loses its natural ability to restrict movement of nutrients through its protective lining. Improper absorption occurs, and the body starts to react to the ingredients slipping into the system. Chemicals called *cytokines* are created, and they circulate throughout the body, causing prolonged inflammation that has been linked to arthritis, heart disease, allergies, and cancer. The immune system, which relies on a healthy intestine, is compromised and becomes imbalanced, often leading to autoimmune diseases and reducing the effectiveness of its normal monitoring abilities.

Dry, processed kibble can also create dehydration, which has been linked to kidney disease in cats. Research indicates that one-third of all indoor cats die of chronic kidney disease. Our pets' bodies are dependent on obtaining most of their water from food. Fresh, wholesome food is high in water content, whereas that of dry kibble is very low or nonexistent. We have been led to believe that pets will compensate for this dehydration by drinking more from their water dish, but this is not the case. It is not normal for a dog or cat to seek out most of its water from a source other than its food. By the time the pet does begin to compensate by going to the water dish more frequently, the kidneys have already been overworked and other tissues have dried out, leading to disease.

When I lecture about pet nutritional needs, I often tell the audience to imagine that they are walking in a beautiful orchard. They stop and pick a fresh, organic apple from the tree and eat it. Then I ask them how they might benefit from this snack. Many people will tell me how they would receive nourishment from the fresh apple, but rarely will anyone offer the deeper, holistic benefit. When we eat a fresh, wholesome apple, we are taking not only nutrients into our bodies but also the vital essence of the apple as well. Life force is combining with life force. The apple has now become one with us not just biochemically, but energetically.

Everything and everyone who played a role in the development of that apple is part of it, and when we take it into our bodies, we are one with all of that creation; it is now part of *us.* This is life experiencing life at many levels. When we feed processed food to our pets or eat it ourselves, we have lost that critical connection and have opted to use a lifeless food to sustain life—a contradiction.

Happy Chefs for Happy Pets

Let's turn our attention now to what I refer to as the *secondary energy input.* That is, the overall energetic balance of food is affected by its exposure to other energy sources.

Imagine yourself eating at a fine restaurant. You've selected a wonderful meal that consists of healthy, wholesome foods, and you expect that you'll benefit from this in many ways. Now, imagine that the person in the kitchen who is preparing your meal has just come to work after having fought with his or her spouse and is in a terrible mood. The negative energy produced due to the emotional upset of the chef is affecting the quality of your food, whether you or the chef is aware of it or not. The energetic components of the wholesome food will be altered by the negative energy that is coming from the emotionally disturbed chef. The net result is *not* the benefit you had planned when you ordered your meal.

I remember several years ago, while visiting a small town in southern British Columbia, Canada, I had been given a recommendation for a restaurant with a great reputation. While I was waiting for my meal, I noticed the door to the kitchen was open. The two chefs were dancing and singing while they were cooking. It filled me with joy to watch those happy people prepare my food, and I wasn't at all surprised to find that my meal was one of the best I had ever eaten.

So, when our intent is to provide the best nutrition available, we *must* consider the source. It is true that many of the farming practices that were standard with the family farms of old have given way to the mass-production options of corporate farms most prevalent in today's society. Corporate farms may use chemicals such as pesticides and herbicides that contaminate our food. Another practice that has become common among food-producing giants, who sacrifice quality nutrition in favor of rapid and abundant production, is genetic modification, along with hormones used to increase growth. In addition, the inhumane handling and treatment of food-producing animals is not only morally unethical but also has a deleterious effect on the quality of the final product. All these practices and many more, the realities of which have been withheld from the public, have deteriorated the quality of the foods essential to our and our pets' existence.

Until we can find a way to end these methods of food production, we have to make a conscious choice to assess all our options when selecting food to consume. We need to take the time to educate ourselves properly, as nutrition is the building block for our bodies and those of our pets as well.

To select the diet that fits our needs, we have to identify our intent. Do we really want to provide a balanced, wholesome diet for our pet, knowing that there will probably be an increase in cost and investment of our personal time? Or are we content to make some sacrifices in the name of convenience?

I enjoy watching my wife prepare food for our pets. She takes the time to assemble a meal for them that is balanced and nutritious. Both of our dogs, Satch' Mo and Chloe, have similar dietary needs that are met with one diet formula. My wife buys ingredients that are wholesome and will opt for organic varieties if possible. Then she puts the food together with the same attitude as the cooks at the little restaurant in Canada. She's aware of the joy she gets when she's providing something so healthy for the pets she loves. She doesn't see it as a burden or as something that deprives her of time that she could be using to do something else. It all comes down to her attitude, and I'm sure that our pets benefit from it greatly.

Don't feel bad if you don't want to prepare your pet's food. It would be better to provide a high-quality commercial pet food than to feel burdened while preparing food yourself. If you do decide to use a commercial pet food, look for one that fits your pet's unique nutritional needs and provides good, wholesome ingredients. Avoid diets high in carbohydrates. Read the ingredient list closely, and avoid grains and unnatural preservatives and additives. Opt for protein sources from meat rather than meat by-products. If this seems too difficult, find a holistic veterinarian and work with him or her in formulating a plan to provide the best diet available for your pet.

As we've seen, selecting a diet from a holistic perspective goes far beyond choosing basic ingredients. And whether we decide to prepare our pets' food with the most nutritious ingredients available or we feed our pet the best commercial diet we can find, we cannot guarantee absolute dietary perfection. We have little control over how the ingredients were grown or how they were handled up until they reached our homes. What we *can* do to help raise the beneficial energy is bless the food before we serve it.

If blessing food seems too "religious" or makes you uncomfortable, then look at it from an energetic angle. From a spiritual perspective, blessing something is an act to bring God's grace into the picture. From an energetic perspective, it's an intent to draw in a pure source of perfect natural energy that will harmonize with the energetic forces of that which is being blessed. From either standpoint, the life force of the object (that is, the food to be served) will be enhanced as a result.

Let's move on to the next chapter, "Minding the Mind and Spirit," to explore this remarkable mind-body relationship further.

CHAPTER EIGHT

MINDING THE MIND AND SPIRIT

"The mind commands the body and the body obeys.
But the mind commands itself, and it is resisted."

— SAINT AUGUSTINE

As recently as 20 years ago, medicine scoffed at the idea that the thought process of the brain could influence the body. Today, however, the mind-body relationship is taught at medical schools throughout the United States and the world.

Because Western medicine is structured on scientific principles, it was impossible to use standard protocols to explain how an energetic factor, such as an emotion, could have an effect on the physical body. The only way to do so was to transcend the barriers of logic. After years of experiments that produced the same results, science finally agreed that the nonmeasurable energies of emotions could have a *predictable* result on the body. Stress does indeed affect the immune system, and an imbalanced immune system can lead to physical disease.

What's more, the holistic community emphasizes the profound influence of factors on physical health that go far beyond the mind.

So let's explore how *both* the realms of mind and spirit affect the well-being of our beloved pets.

The Energy of Thoughts

Thoughts are energy, and energy is manifested in different ways according to its dimensional form. Mindful or intuitive thoughts are higher on the dimensional scale than rational thoughts or emotions. When we are mindful or aware enough to receive intuitive thoughts, we are interacting with source energy—the purest energy there is—which flows from the highest dimensions. Reasoning and emotions are born of mind chatter, essentially the product of energy distortion. When we're trying to solve a problem or we're really angry about something, we're not aware of the source energy. Worse, the energy of those kinds of thoughts is disrupting the source energy flowing through us (which, again, explains why thoughts and emotions can affect our health).

Both rational thinking and emotions can be directly related to brain function and are wired as patterns of electrical impulses. For example, scientists have performed experiments in which certain parts of subjects' brains are stimulated, and the stimulation triggers memories the subjects aren't even aware they had. It's all in there somewhere.

We're designed so that certain rational thoughts create neuronal loops, and these act like thought reflexes so we can maximize the speed of our responses to recurring situations. For example, say you're driving down the road when another car suddenly pulls out in front of you, almost causing an accident. Without direct conscious control, you automatically respond by applying your foot to the brake pedal and pushing it down as quickly as possible. You might turn the steering wheel to avoid the collision. The fear of a near collision creates an automatic emotional response of anger, and you begin to yell at the other driver. Both the thought processes of adjustments in your driving and the emotional response based on a fearful reaction are due to *patterns* that exist in the brain to maximize the efficiency of your response. It takes less energy for this automation to occur than if you directed each of these reactions independently.

When we have persistent or recurring negative thoughts or emotions that create negative energy, the result is a resistance or alteration of the normal directive energy that manifests as the physical body. This is how our thoughts or emotions can potentially create physical disease. If the resistance is removed, the harmonious flow will resume, and the body will return to a state of well-being.

Pet Constitutions

Emotional effects on the body and stress can cause imbalance in the immune system. Both Traditional Chinese Medicine and Ayurveda, practiced in India, consider emotional balance paramount in maintaining health. According to the Chinese, all individuals fall into five basic elements or constitutions: *Fire, Earth, Metal, Water,* and *Wood.* Each of the constitutions has a dominant organ associated with it: When animals or humans with a particular constitution are strong, the corresponding dominant organ serves them well, but when they are out of balance, it becomes their weak link.

For example, a pet with the Water constitution is dominated by the kidney, a yin organ, as well as the balancing yang organ, the urinary bladder. A Water-constitution pet will display the emotion of fear when there is imbalance in these organs. But the influential pathway runs both ways. If the Water-constitution pet is subjected to fearful emotions for extended periods of time, there is the strong potential of developing kidney or urinary bladder disease.

When we know our pets' constitution, we can accurately predict what the physical and emotional outcomes will be if they become imbalanced for prolonged periods. This is an enormous aid when it comes to preventing disease. If we know what things will lead to imbalance and avoid them, choose diets that are constitutionally balancing, and offer routine complementary balancing protocols, we can prevent many of the "untreatable" diseases that often occur within the conventional health paradigm.

For your reference, here's a very simple chart outlining each of the five constitutions and their corresponding issues.

Fire: Dominated by the heart. When in balance, pets with a Fire constitution are characterized by:

- Happiness being the center of attention
- Readiness to perform to cheer up or attract others
- Affectionate behavior, including licking your face or rubbing against you
- An enjoyment of fun and the urge to seek more
- Being the life of the party

When out of balance, pets with a Fire constitution are just completely manic. Their energetic and playful personality seems almost desperate and can become intrusive, even aggressive. They may also suffer from heart conditions.

Earth: Dominated by the spleen or gastrointestinal system. When in balance, pets with an Earth constitution are characterized by:

- Groundedness and unflappability
- An easygoing, relaxed nature
- An ability to take everything in stride

When out of balance, pets with an Earth constitution will seem tense, worried, and pensive. They may also suffer from digestive problems, especially acid reflux or irritable bowel disorder.

Metal: Dominated by the lungs and upper intestines. When in balance, pets with a Metal constitution are characterized by:

- An urge to look for a task or responsibility to perform
- A consciousness of borders and need to set boundaries
- A focus on maintaining order

- An often angular appearance (greyhounds, for example)

When out of balance, pets with a Metal constitution often display signs of grief, along with upper-respiratory infections, asthma, or lung disease, as well as chronic constipation.

Water: Dominated by the kidneys and bladder. When in balance, pets with Water constitutions are characterized by:

- Loving, nurturing dispositions

- A loyal and almost clingy nature

- Strong territorial and protective behavior

When out of balance, pets with a Water constitution typically suffer from timidity and will display fearful behavior. They are also predisposed to kidney disease and urinary tract infections.

Wood: Dominated by the liver. When in balance, pets with a Wood constitution are characterized by:

- Lots of drive and ambition

- Strong emotions

- A desire to be in charge or lead others

- A tendency to bring out the spark in others

- Boldness

When out of balance, pets with a Wood constitution can become easily frustrated, especially if they aren't able to get or maintain control, and that frustration often turns into anger over time. Because the unbalanced liver is believed to generate excess amounts of heat in the body, unbalanced Wood-constitution pets may suffer from what the Chinese consider heat-related illnesses, such as infections in the skin or ears, seizures, and cancer.

Balancing the Emotions

Jackson had been the beloved family dog for nine years, ever since puppyhood. The confident cairn terrier, according to his caretakers, had always had a "mind of his own," but no matter what, he'd loved his caretakers' two children profusely as he and the family grew together. Now Jackson had come to me because his family believed they were at their wit's end. The family's only pet, he had become angry and had bitten the kids on more than one occasion. His regular veterinarian had addressed his aggressive behavior by prescribing two behavior-modification drugs and a nonsteroidal anti-inflammatory medication, in the event that pain was causing Jackson's aggressiveness. They were also told to keep the children away from Jackson to prevent the possibility of further biting incidents. Nothing seemed to be working, and the caretakers were considering euthanasia to protect the children.

After thoroughly questioning the caretakers, I gave Jackson a physical examination that included a holistic approach, taking into account aspects such as pulse characteristic, tongue quality, active acupuncture points, nutrition and environmental factors, and a constitutional assessment. Because of his "alpha dog" personality and self-confidence, it was obvious to me that Jackson was a Wood-constitution dog and, thus, under the influence of the liver. His behavioral problems reinforced my assessment, since I knew that an imbalanced liver will emotionally manifest as anger and aggression.

I treated the acupuncture points that would correct his imbalances, prescribed a Chinese herb that would continue to harmonize the liver, and altered his diet to reduce his carbohydrate intake. In a short while, Jackson was his old self, and the aggressive behavior subsided. He was monitored for liver imbalances, and with the diet modification and intermittent herbal supplements, he resumed his normal, happy life.

If we are aware of the influence of emotions on the body, we can direct our attention to balancing them as a means of preventing physical disease. If our pet begins to display imbalanced emotions, as indicated by a dramatic change in behavior like Jackson's or an otherwise clear emergence of a dominant negative emotion, we should look for possible constitutional causes. Chronic problems, in particular, are often signs of an imbalance related to the pet's constitution.

For example, at the clinic, we're routinely confronted with cats brought in for inappropriately urinating in the house. We will often investigate whether something has changed in the environment and find out that the family might have a new child or pet. We assume that the cat is irritated and vengeful and has been urinating in inappropriate places to get back at them. This may be the case, but we must also consider the possibility that the cat is afraid of the new addition to the family, and the fear manifests as a urinary bladder imbalance. It's reasonable to give the cat something that will modify the behavior, but addressing the imbalance of the urinary bladder will often prevent further problems down the road.

In another similar example, consider one of the most common sources of irritation for the caretaker of an outside dog: digging in the yard. All sorts of techniques have been tried to stop the behavior. They range from putting water, balloons, or even hot peppers in the holes to covering them with dirt in hopes of discouraging the dog from digging.

Dr. Bonnie Beaver, a veterinarian at Texas A&M University, is a pioneering specialist in the understanding of pet behavior. She explained that if caretakers would take the time to identify *where* the dog was digging, then they could identify *why* the dog was digging:

- If the holes were near the back door of the house, the dog likely wanted to go inside.

- If the holes were near the fence, the dog probably wanted to leave the property to find a companion.

- If the holes were randomly dug throughout the yard, the dog was most likely getting in the holes to cool him- or herself.

If the caretaker becomes aware of the emotional disturbance or desire that initiated the digging, then the chance of eliminating the problem will be greatly increased. This is a much better option than finding the dog a new home or giving him or her to the animal shelter for adoption.

Treat the Caretaker, Treat the Pet

Midnight was a middle-aged domestic shorthair cat with an ongoing skin disease. He had been seen by his regular veterinarian over the past year, but his skin problem would not resolve. He was brought to my office in hopes that alternative treatments might help.

Midnight spent most of his awake time grooming himself excessively. In time his skin became inflamed, and scabs appeared over most of his body. His black fur fell out in bunches, leaving the poor cat looking like a moth-eaten creature with crusty skin.

Over the next three months, I treated Midnight with acupuncture and Chinese herbs and also changed his diet. Nothing seemed to help. Midnight's caretaker, Jess, was patient with my failures, and she never complained. One afternoon Midnight came in for a reexamination, and a man whom I did not know was in the exam room. I was introduced to Nick, Jess's husband.

I began to apologize to Nick for not solving Midnight's skin problem. He interrupted me and said, "You don't have to apologize to me. I have the same thing going on myself." He stood up and lifted his shirt. His entire stomach had the same appearance as Midnight's skin. He added, "My doctors can't seem to find out what my skin problem is, either."

The gentleman went on to explain that, over the past year, he had been to several specialists, and no one could help resolve the problem. The best-guess diagnosis they had to offer was "neurological dermatitis," essentially a stress-induced skin condition, and he was being treated with steroids.

Recognizing their similar skin condition not only demonstrated the energetic connection between Midnight and his caretaker that caused the condition to persist, but allowed me to take its emotional component into consideration. The negative emotional energy being carried by the caretaker and picked up by the pet was creating physical changes that were harming the skin of both. Medications were helping alleviate symptoms but were not addressing the underlying root problem, which in this case was related not to Midnight's constitution so much as to the energy from the negative emotions in his environment. To resolve the disease and return to a normal, healthy state would require resolving the emotional problems that, again, were coming from the caretaker.

Why do negative emotions express themselves in precisely this type of skin disorder? I've asked myself that many times and, as of yet, have no answers. I suspect it may have to do with an individual's unique makeup. Perhaps Midnight's caretaker had a genetic predisposition toward dermatitis or a "weak link" such that, when he was thrown out of balance, it manifested as a skin condition rather than something else.

However, it's important to know that the manifestation of imbalances or distorted energy (that is, negative emotions) can express itself in two general ways. Midnight's situation was a clear case of *mirroring,* when the pet's emotional and/or physical state directly mimics that of his human companion. But not all cases of energetic disturbance flowing from caretaker to pet manifest in such an obvious way. When there are prolonged emotional problems going on in the pet's environment, the pet will not always take on the same emotional disorder. Instead, the imbalance could be expressed by affecting the pet's "weak link" in his or her constitutional predisposition for illness.

For instance, persistent anger in the home does not necessarily cause the pet to become angry. Nor does it mean that, in every case, if a caretaker is suffering from a physical ailment, a pet will suffer the same condition. I have seen many animal patients over the years that displayed physical symptoms directly related to the emotional disturbance coming from the caretaker, and not all were cases of mirroring.

Change the Environment, Change the Pet

For another example of the clear emotional connection between pet and caretaker, let me tell you about my patient Tommy. Since the time he had arrived at the clinic as a feisty kitten, he seemed intent on taking his anger out on his caretakers. Over the years, Tommy became inexplicably enraged at his people and would often attack and bite them. As difficult as it was to live with Tommy, they refused to give up on him and tolerated his emotional outbursts.

I spent a great deal of time with Tommy, trying to ascertain the root of his imbalance so I could help right it. I focused on every possible perspective and attempted everything I knew to reestablish an emotional equilibrium that would make Tommy's life better. Knowing extreme anger can be an expression of an imbalanced Metal constitution, I treated Tommy with certain herbal supplements, which would improve his disposition only temporarily. In time he would return to his old angry self.

One day I received a phone call from one of Tommy's caretakers, Doug. He informed me that sadly he and his wife had divorced and that he alone would be taking care of Tommy. I tried to console him, knowing that the divorce might cause the cat to become even more aggressive.

However, this did not happen. About six months after the phone call, Tommy came in to the clinic for a routine procedure. Doug told me that Tommy had calmed down and no longer displayed the aggressive behavior that had haunted his life. He now slept on the bed and spent his time purring and rubbing against his caretaker.

I was very happy to get this report and couldn't help asking Doug, "Do you mind me asking you what type of relationship you and your wife had?"

Doug responded, "Oh, it was not good. We fought all the time. You know, like cats and dogs."

Though it certainly happens that our pets may suffer from an imbalance that doesn't stem from us, as responsible caretakers we simply cannot overlook these crucial things:

- The importance of the emotions and subsequent *physical* diseases

- The importance of physical diseases and subsequent *emotional* imbalances

- The effects that *our* emotional imbalances have on the emotions and bodies of our *pets*

If we recognize the energetic connection between us and our pets—and accept that it affects the physical bodies of both—then we can use this knowledge in holistically approaching health care and our animals' well-being.

If negative energy comes from the caretaker to the pet and results in physical disease, then perhaps positive energy from the caretaker can assist in healing the pet. This is something I've been focused on for the past few years in my practice, and the results have been promising. Moreover, I've given a lot of thought to how we can take preventive measures, supporting well-being for ourselves and our pets in the process.

For several years, the medical community has acknowledged the benefits of practices like meditation, yoga, and tai chi in helping reduce stress, depression, and anxiety; lower blood pressure; and relieve chronic pain. All these ancient practices eliminate mind chatter and other distractions and allow us to focus our awareness on our internal states of being, improving our ability to resolve issues that may be causing us pain, such as negative thought patterns and emotions. The condition of the internal self directly influences our external condition, or our physical self.

Ultimately, anything we can do to help harmonize body, mind, and spirit will benefit our energetic body, and that will influence our physical health. This in turn benefits our pets by exposing them to a healthier energetic environment—not to mention a happier, calmer caretaker!

The Divine Pathway of the Spirit

Imagine spotting a sick or injured animal on the roadside in a desolate location. You are immediately filled with empathy. At that moment, driven by compassion, you exhibit behavior that you've never before displayed. Maybe you leave your car and follow the animal into the woods, tossing aside all fears, hoping to provide help. You might find the animal, or you might not. But the animal has provided an experience that has benefited you, the human. You might now summon up this experience to embolden you at times when you become fearful. This is part of the animal's divine purpose.

In my work with animal communicators, pets have told me that they served a purpose in their human caretakers' lives and informed me that they selected their humans based on that purpose, perhaps occupying a role that will provide us with an experience that we might need, as in the above example. A more common example is eliciting love in the form of the tremendous grief most people feel with the loss of a beloved pet. It is not hard to imagine that a child experiencing this grief can learn a great lesson about love.

In my 30-plus years of practicing veterinary medicine, I've seen many people who are unable to open themselves up to love or to be loved by others, yet they find that they can open their hearts to their pets and experience a profound, unconditional love that they might never encounter with another human.

But where does this purpose come from? Who gave the pet this mission, so to speak? As we've already discussed, at a higher level of awareness or consciousness, the illusion of separation between individuals disappears and a oneness exists. At this elevated dimension, the source energy from which we originate is revealed to be the same source of *all* beings. As the energy filters down to the physical dimension we inhabit, it retains information and guidance from the source. This *divine pathway,* as it is often referred to in holistic circles, is what really controls all bodily function down to the structure of our genetic code. Pets have a divine pathway as well, directed by the same source as ours. So, it is not surprising that we are guided to cross each other's paths and share experiences along the way.

I am confident that many of our pets come into our lives with a specific purpose, guided by the information encoded into their spirits by source energy. And *you* are probably already helping your pet satisfy that purpose, without even realizing it. Many of us are moved to share our lives with pets. This inclination, or heartfelt sense, is itself an expanded state of consciousness. Perhaps that is our divine path trying to steer us in the right direction for our own spiritual growth—to a pet whose own divine path is steering *him* toward us.

Realigning with Source Energy

This book is geared toward helping you shift your understanding of the connection between you and your pet so that both of you can benefit emotionally, mentally, physically, and spiritually. When you focus your attention on the energetic bond between you and your animal companions, you automatically realign yourself with your source energy and begin to heal immediately.

Imagine that you've had a stressful day at work. You're exhausted when you arrive at home that evening, and you make yourself a frozen dinner and plop down in front of the television to unwind. Whether you know it or not, the stressful energy that you brought home with you is affecting not only you but *everything* in your environment, including your pet. If this persists, day after day, then the accumulated effects of the negative energy can cause disease in you both.

Now imagine that you come home from work after having a stressful day and instead of finding a comfortable chair and escaping with the television, you spend fifteen minutes with your pet. You focus your attention on the gratitude you have for him being there for you, cuddle or stroke him, and tell him how much you appreciate him. You notice that your spirits start to lift, and you begin to feel better. You go to bed relaxed, and awaken with more energy to face the upcoming day.

By tapping into the energetic bond between you and your pet, and creating loving, caring feelings, you've energized your body by aligning with source energy. A coherence forms—just like two pendulums synchronizing themselves—that will realign you with healing and well-being.

Our pets are intuitively aware of their source energy; when we focus on the energetic bond between us and them, we can find the same intuitive awareness and connect with our own. We're swept to a higher level of consciousness, well-being flows like a river through our essence, and a vital influx of perfect energy and healing occurs at all levels. We've moved ourselves back in alignment with our divine pathway. When we nourish our spirit, we will inevitably nourish our pets' as well, through our connection.

Many spiritual teachers throughout history have said that source energy is love, and love is source. I believe that this is true. Love is not about the fleeting emotions that wax and wane over the course of relationships; rather, it is the deepest feeling of all. It is that light that shines in all of us, and it is our pathway back to source. It's where all of creation begins, and nothing has ever existed without it. It's our "port in the stormy sea" and our direction back to ourselves. When we find ways to reconnect to our source as love, the barriers come down and well-being flows, bathing us in its radiance and pouring out to all those around us. This is where miracles happen and where healing has no limitations.

When we focus on our energetic connection to our pets, and we let ourselves start *feeling* instead of thinking, the love that reveals itself reconnects us with our source—and balance and well-being begin to be restored. And in time, when the feeling subsides and thoughts move us back into our physical reality, we find ourselves in a higher state of clarity. We begin to see things from a new perspective of loving compassion. We realize that this state of joy is what life was intended to be.

When you experience the clarity of the higher self, the barriers that separate you from others—including your pet—start to fall away, and obstacles are removed. As you reap the wonderful benefits of this existence, so does your faithful animal companion.

CHAPTER NINE

COMPLEMENTARY
MODALITIES

*"To make the patient better before taking
the medicine is the most direct method."*

— ATTRIBUTED TO XU SHU-WEI

Complementary or alternative modalities (also known as CAM) for treating disease and promoting healing have gained popularity in the West—and this trend is new and exciting! Here in the United States, people are becoming aware of these approaches and are drawn to them in hopes of expanding their health-care options. The movement toward complementary modalities is increasingly prevalent. In the fall of 2012, *Time* magazine published a special edition devoted entirely to alternative medicine. In addition, the National Center for Complementary and Integrative Health was formed in 1998 to research alternative modalities, and in 2001, the Mayo Clinic launched their Complementary and Integrative Medicine Program.

The same holds true for veterinary medicine, as more and more veterinary hospitals are extending their services to include one or more of these options. People are looking for healthier, more natural methods of treatment, and they are in turn compelling clinicians, both in human and veterinary medicine, to look beyond the rigid boundaries of Western practices and consider other methods.

Although the idea of using complementary or alternative modalities seems new, most methods are very old. Many of them have been used in other countries for hundreds of years and, in fact, are the go-to methods for promoting and maintaining good health. As I mentioned earlier, Traditional Chinese Medicine has been used for more than 3,000 years, and there has been recent evidence that it might go back much further. Likewise, Ayurvedic medicine has been in use for millennia as one of the primary methodologies of medical treatment in India. Only recently have the boundaries of Western medicine been breached by these ancient methods, and this has been the direct result of people seeking alternatives to the limitations and downsides of traditional Western medicine.

Not long ago I attended a veterinary conference and listened to a presenter speak about a new technology for treating cancer patients. This renowned research veterinarian, who has spent many years studying cancer in both animals and humans, was excited and enthusiastic when he described a method of removing the energetic components of chemotherapeutic drugs and inserting them into water or saline and giving the patient the remedy, therefore providing the benefits of the drug treatment while eliminating the negative side effects. This sounded like *Star Wars* technology to most of the professional clinicians listening, but what he described utilizes the *same* energetic principles that have been used by homeopaths for thousands of years.

Indeed, among these alternative therapies based on ancient philosophies, some exciting and groundbreaking techniques are backed by the latest scientific research. In this chapter, I'll introduce several complementary modalities, including:

- Energy medicine
- Acupuncture and Chinese herbal therapy (the treatment methodology in Traditional Chinese Medicine)
- Chiropractic care
- Homeopathy and homotoxicology
- Ayurvedic medicine

I refer to these modalities as "complementary" because ideally they would be used in addition to, rather than instead of, Western techniques. I want to stress the importance of always adopting the approach that is in the *best* interest of the pet. Time and again I meet caretakers who believe that Western medicine is bad and who only want an alternative solution. To me, this attitude is no different from the attitude of those who turn their noses up at the thought of promoting healing with complementary modalities. Extremes at both ends of the spectrum do not serve the pet.

So, how do we decide if we should seek out a complementary practitioner when looking for a veterinarian? A veterinarian who practices integrative medicine, one who offers both traditional Western medicine as well as complementary modalities, has a distinct advantage over either a strictly traditional Western veterinarian or one who employs only alternative modalities. When I talk to groups of pet caretakers about health and healing, I like to remind them that if a dog with an arrow sticking out of his side arrives at my clinic, I will remove the arrow with surgery. I will not place acupuncture needles in the dog to "treat" the arrow, nor will I send him home with herbal remedies in hopes that the arrow might fall out. I'm in favor of doing what is in the *best* interest of the pet, and I'll use any therapy available to help.

When I practiced Western medicine exclusively and I would treat a dog with persistent epileptic seizures, the only option I had was to put the dog on medications to control the seizures. If the same dog were presented to me now, I would most likely treat my patient with acupuncture and Chinese herbal remedies, aiming to not only control the symptoms but also eliminate the source of the problem (in this case, the seizures are the symptoms).

However, it's crucial to remain open to all types of available therapy. For instance, I remember being presented with Josie, a sick golden retriever that had seen her regular veterinarian, who focused strictly on Western medicine. Josie had been ill for several days and had not responded to her veterinarian's treatment. It just so happened that I had worked with Josie and her caretakers many years prior to my starting my own practice, so they told their veterinarian they were going to see if I could help the dog using one of my complementary modalities. The vet's response was, "Well, if you want to go over there and deal with voodoo, that's fine. But I'm doing *real* medicine here." Not to be dissuaded, they came to me with the expectation that, since traditional medicine hadn't helped Josie, I would offer an alternative approach.

Now, as a holistic veterinarian, I look at all angles for every patient. When I examined Josie, I found a large swelling in her abdomen. I then reviewed her history and discovered that she'd never been spayed. I decided that I should do some further testing. When I did, I became convinced that the swelling was Josie's enlarged, infected uterus and that it was about to rupture. At that moment, I went to her caretakers and explained that I wouldn't be doing acupuncture or sending home herbs—if we didn't go into surgery and get the uterus out before it ruptured, Josie would die. They were surprised, but agreed. We did the surgery, and Josie came out just fine. The takeaway here is that this wasn't even a case of Western versus complementary medicine; rather, it was taking all perspectives into account to determine the best course of action and staying open to all options. In this case, Josie's underlying problem required surgical intervention, and merely treating the patient's pattern imbalances with acupuncture and Chinese herbs or even with the other vet's protocol wasn't the solution.

Complementary or alternative modalities for treating illness and promoting healing are tools to add to my toolbox of remedies. The more tools I have at my disposal, the more likely I am to find an option that will satisfy my intention. If I have several options to treat the same condition, I can select the one that will best promote healing with the fewest side effects and the lowest cost. If I'm limited to just one modality, then I've reduced my options and narrowed the outcome for the pet and caretaker. Remember, a holistic approach to medicine is one that considers the whole—and that does not mean excluding the tremendous benefits that Western medicine has to offer.

Understanding the Differences in Approach

To appreciate the advantages of complementary modalities, let's look at some of the fundamental differences between traditional

Western medicine and other types of medicine. To recap what we've already learned, Western medicine is based on scientific principles that have been proven in the laboratory. It's primarily based on the assumption that the body is a biological entity composed of a dense mass of organic compounds controlled by chemical processes. Science has spent many years determining how the body works biochemically, both in a normal state and when disease causes it to deviate from normal.

In Western medicine, methods for preventing and treating disease have been derived from those same scientific beliefs, and this explains why disease-fighting therapies primarily use chemical compounds (such as those found in pharmaceuticals). The use of pharmaceuticals to treat disease has been tremendously successful but has not come without problems. It's very difficult to introduce a drug into the body that will *only* affect the diseased part. Hence, the long lists of side effects that often accompany medications. Most of us know that chemotherapy has the potential to kill not only cancer cells but also normal cells. But not all of us are aware that, in reality, most of the drugs we put in our bodies have side effects.

For example, antibiotics have been effectively used for many years in the treatment of bacterial infections. However, we're just now learning about the long-term effects of antibiotics on the body. Research has shown that not only do antibiotics damage and destroy the normal, necessary bacteria that reside in the body, but they also compromise the immune system—our natural ability to fight disease—for many years to come. Strong evidence suggests that the more often a patient has received antibiotics throughout life, the higher the risk of developing certain cancers.

Similarly, the use of immunization therapy has been scrutinized and questioned in veterinary medicine. It appears that the standard vaccination protocols for dogs and cats for many years may be overzealous. Many researchers believe that annual vaccination programs may lead to immune imbalance and potential autoimmune disease. New three-year vaccination protocols used for core diseases in dogs and cats have proven to be just as protective as yearly shots, and they minimize the risks involved with immune imbalance.

Many times over the years, I have seen pharmaceutical companies rush to make claims that their newest drug is safe and effective. As a young veterinarian, I witnessed the ability of powerful drug manufacturers to sidestep protocols that had been instituted to protect pets from harmful side effects. At the time, all our vaccines for rabies were given by intramuscular injection. The protocol was to give 1 cc of the vaccine to any size dog or cat in the muscle. Unfortunately, in the case of a small dog or cat, the pet would experience a great deal of pain and would often limp around for hours or days. This was something that neither the pet nor the caretaker enjoyed.

It isn't hard to imagine that when one of the leading pharmaceutical companies developed the first rabies vaccine that could be injected under the skin instead of into the muscle, most veterinarians were overjoyed. Hoping to eliminate the pain associated with the old intramuscular vaccines, veterinarians immediately purchased the new type and began administering it. Several months later, the same pharmaceutical company was forced to recall the vaccine, as it had been found to be inadequate in protecting the animals against the disease. The drug company had been given a "temporary" permit to market the vaccine until the final clinical trials were completed. Veterinarians were forced to contact each client whose pet had recently received a rabies vaccination to break the news that the first one hadn't been effective and the pet would have to be revaccinated.

One of the major differences between Western medicine and other, complementary modalities is that the philosophy in the West is based on treating the disease instead of the individual patient. It reasons that if one patient has a known disease and his or her body works to destroy the disease, then the body of another patient will respond to the disease in the same way. With this logic, it can be assumed that if a certain drug is effective at fighting a particular disease in one patient, then it will most likely be so in all patients. This would be handy for the clinician and beneficial for the drug manufacturer; however, research is only just now recognizing that this idea is not valid.

If we accept the generalization principle for diseases, then we must accept that the underlying reason for development of that disease is identical for all patients and, therefore, the results of a specific treatment will be as well. This assumption ignores individuality and explains why treatment options in Western medicine for each disease are extremely limited.

†

So now that you have a solid understanding of how complementary medicine fits into the broader picture of caring for your pet, let's look in more detail at a few of the most common types of healing modalities you'll encounter in the world of holistic healing.

Intuition and Energy Healing

First, let me make it clear that whether we choose to treat a sick pet with a traditional pharmaceutical compound or use a complementary approach such as acupuncture or homeopathy, ultimately we are using energy to alter energy. Even our standard pills and tablets are composed of swirling energy. At some time in the future, as scientists learn more and more about the subatomic reality of the body, we clinicians will be able to select more exact modalities that promote the energy of healing.

I use the term *energy medicine* because it helps us focus on the underlying premise that all things are ultimately made up of energy, and it reminds us of our lessons in quantum physics. Whether it is a bouncing cocker-spaniel puppy or a couch potato of a calico cat, every animal, plant, and mineral that exists consists of swirling energy.

Energy healers are often people gifted with the ability to receive intuitive messages. As we've discussed, one function of the right hemisphere of the brain is receiving intuitive thoughts or guidance. This can be difficult in a clinical situation, as our rational thinking will usually dominate and prevent the subtle messages from the intuitive mind from getting through. But some people can tune out their reasoning brain and tune in to their intuitive mind at will, or at least with more ease.

The higher-dimensional intuitive mind allows the energy healer to tap into information that's improbable to obtain with normal thought process, information from energy and things we cannot readily "see" or measure. In particular, information received by the intuitive mind can help locate energetic—as well as emotional, mental, and spiritual—imbalances in the body. The information that the healers receive might come in the form of a feeling or a picture, or it could be a thought or "voice" they become aware of and from which they receive guidance.

Once the intuitive information is received, there can be a shift in consciousness to a more targeted form of healing. The clinician who directs the healing will focus on an intention to correct the imbalance, knowing that healing is controlled at a higher dimension. Remember, three conditions are required: *intention, focus,* and *belief.*

It can be hard for us to imagine that it is possible to direct healing with our minds, because the healing takes place at an energy dimension that's higher than our perception. But consider all you've learned about the true nature of our beings and our relationship to one another on the energetic level. People are able to move their consciousness to higher dimensions where there are *no boundaries* between them and the receiver of the healing. This is also why an intuitive can work on a patient (human or animal) when they're in different geographic locations.

Reiki

One of the first energetic modalities introduced to the West was Reiki. Considered a holistic form of treatment, it emphasizes the balancing of mind, body, and spirit, and recognizes that imbalance in any one of these creates disease (or dis-ease). Reiki was developed in Japan in 1922 by a Buddhist monk named Mikao Usui. During a spiritual experience, Usui was given a healing energy through his seventh chakra, which is the body's energetic center that communicates with spirit, in order to promote healing in people.

Reiki practitioners believe that Reiki energy is derived from universal life energy, or spiritual energy. Therefore, it is pure, perfect, and unlimited. Reiki is not "taught." Rather, it's passed from a Reiki master to the student in an attunement process. Then the student learns how to direct the healing energy to the patient, usually applying his or her hands to the patient's body in specific locations used for healing the whole body or just in those that need balancing. Master Reiki practitioners often say that they are guided by "intuitive feelings."

Having been through the attunement process myself, I've used Reiki on my animal patients for many years, and it has certainly helped direct healing. A close friend and Reiki instructor lived next to our clinic and would come over each morning to perform Reiki healing on all the sick pets in the hospital, as well as those recovering from surgery. It was a rewarding experience watching her work, and I'm positive that the pets benefited greatly.

I'm reminded of a story my Reiki master told me. She and her sister, another Reiki practitioner, would help with an annual event at a local ranch that brought together children with special needs and horses—typically older ones that were extremely safe for the children to ride. As one would expect, these geriatric horses had a variety of chronic pain issues. My Reiki master explained that these horses could feel the healing energy coming from her and her sister; the animals would approach them and lean their bodies against the Reiki practitioners exactly at their points of pain. Imagine two women in a pasture with a small group of horses all pushing their way to get in contact with the gifts of healing energy. Remarkable!

Biofeedback

Biofeedback—used for both humans and animals—is a modality that has been around in Europe for a while but is relatively new in the United States. Biofeedback is based on the belief that the body's cells communicate via energetic pathways and that disease is associated with interference of this cell communication. Researchers contend that each disease condition has a vibrational pattern that distorts the normal energetic pattern of the body. A biofeedback machine detects the energetic profile of each disease or toxin in the body and then creates an energetic pattern that will neutralize or offset it.

The corrective energetic pattern is usually placed in a water solution much like a homeopathic remedy, and the pet is given the solution orally over a period of time. The energetic treatment can also be delivered via a small chip placed inside the collar, and will then be available to the pet 24 hours a day. Although this form of treatment might seem a bit far-out, from an energetic standpoint it seems to have substance, and the veterinarians I know who are using this modality claim to have great success.

Traditional Chinese Medicine

Throughout history, the Chinese knew that their strength as warriors was limited not only by their own health but also by that of their horses. Thus, Traditional Chinese Medicine became the primary healing modality in humans *and* animals. There are many differences between TCM and our Western medicine, but the principal difference is that TCM does not focus on a disease as the cause of health problems. Practitioners of TCM believe that good health is determined by whether the body is in balance. An imbalance leads to improper health, which they describe as patterns.

TCM is based on several theories, including the *Zang-Fu theory,* which identifies major organs in the body and their interconnections. According to the Chinese, there are five Zang organs (also called *yin* organs) and six Fu organs (also called *yang* organs), connected by en-ergetic pathways, or *meridians,* that can be accessed by acupuncture points, which lie just beneath the skin's surface. The organ system serves to keep the essential energies in a balanced state for optimal function. Energy is called *Qi* (also spelled "Chi") and is found in sev-eral forms in the body:

- **Jing** and **Yuan Qi** are considered congenital energy and are responsible for our development.

- The body also has acquired Qi such as **Gu Qi,** which is energy derived from food.

- **Zong Qi** is the energy that comes from breathing air.

- **Wei Qi** is responsible for the body's defense.

For the body to thrive, there must be balance in the Zang-Fu system as well as normal production and flow of Qi and blood. If something disrupts this balance, disease occurs. The imbalances produce patterns, to which TCM clinicians direct treatment. If the patterns are restored to a normal, balanced system, the disease is considered healed.

For example, a diagnosis of malignant lymphoma (a type of cancer) in a traditional Western veterinary practice would be diagnosed in a practice that offers TCM as an underlying pattern of blood stasis. Instead of administering chemotherapy to attack the cancer, a TCM-trained veterinarian would probably use acupuncture and Chinese herbs to move the blood and resolve the stasis, thereby balancing the patient's system so the pet can heal him- or herself.

Healing and Quality of Life Through TCM

I used to work with a colleague who treated many pets with cancer. He would routinely use harsh chemotherapeutic drugs to fight the disease. I'd work with him to provide an integrative approach that combined traditional Western therapy and TCM, using acupuncture and Chinese herbs. Many of the chemotherapy drugs had severe side effects, including destroying the body's white blood cells. During chemotherapy, monitoring of the patient's white cell count was required, and if the cell numbers dropped below a certain level, then treatment would have to be discontinued. Unfortunately, this occurred in most patients with lymphoma who received chemotherapy.

From a TCM perspective, chemotherapy itself creates a significant imbalance in the body. Therefore, veterinary acupuncturists must work on reestablishing balance associated with the primary cause of the cancer, as well as the imbalance created by the chemotherapy. There are acupuncture points throughout the pet's body that stimulate the production of cancer-fighting cells and can decrease nausea and counter other side effects. By using the integrative approach on these patients, we were able to eliminate many of the side effects, keep the animals eating and active, and reduce much of the pain

associated with the harsh medications. Quality of life, as well as longevity, improved.

Allow me to share the story of Molly, a lovely chow-mix dog. Molly came to the clinic with a definitive diagnosis made by the cancer specialist at the state veterinary college. She had a solid tumor in her brain that had been specifically identified by a biopsy and had received confirmation at the university laboratory. Molly was placed on an oral chemotherapy that had several harsh side effects.

Molly's caretakers, Alan and Javier, had hoped that complemen-
tary treatment might offer her a better prognosis and quality of life. They were told that she had a life expectancy of two months. When I did my initial examination on Molly, she would take two or three steps and then do a somersault and land on her side, unable to get up. The large tumor in her brain had interfered with her ability to walk normally.

Alan, Javier, and I discussed some basic fundamental differences between traditional Western medicine and TCM. We focused on the concept of balance and imbalance, instead of using the word *cancer*. I also asked them to concentrate on healing—specifically the body's brilliant ability to heal itself—and to set aside the fears associated with the poor prognosis that their oncologist had offered.

After a thorough TCM diagnostic exam and identification of the underlying imbalances, we started a twice-weekly series of acupuncture treatments aimed at restoring balance, modulating im-
munity, and reducing the side effects of the chemotherapy. I also suggested two Chinese herbal remedies to dissolve the tumor, a diet change that lowered carbohydrate levels (as previously mentioned, high-carbohydrate diets are linked to cancer growth), and supplements to benefit the immune system.

In two months, Molly and her caretakers returned to the oncologist at the veterinary college for a reevaluation. She was walking normally and doing very well overall. The oncologist was pleasantly surprised, and when asked if they should continue giving the oral chemotherapy, she said that she wasn't sure, as no other patients who had this form of cancer had ever lived this long. Molly continued to surprise the oncologist as she lived symptom-free for another 16 months. (When we started Molly's treatment, she was 14 years old.)

Five Elements Theory

Another component of Traditional Chinese Medicine is the *five elements theory* and the balance of yin and yang. In ancient China, great focus was placed on nature and its harmony. Accordingly, the material world was thought to be composed of five basic elements, and the yin-yang balance depended on the harmony between the components. Those five elements—*Fire, Earth, Metal, Water,* and *Wood*—correspond to the pet constitutions we discussed in Chapter Eight. Recall that each element has distinguishing characteristics and also has a particular and predictable effect when balanced or imbalanced.

Yin energy represents the feminine energy of the earth and is moist, cool, and nourishing, while yang energy represents the male energy of the sun and is dry, warm, and powerful. When yin and yang are in balance, there is harmony and health. If there is imbalance between yin and yang, then patterns begin to emerge and disease will often follow. The trained clinician will identify these imbalances and implement corrective tools that will help reestablish the energetic balance required for good health.

Most TCM clinicians understand that each of the five elements have specific characteristics that have an effect on the body. Every person or pet has a constitution or personality determined by his or her individual dominating element. To recap, here are examples of pets of each element:

- The happy-go-lucky poodle that loves to be the center of attention and wants to always lick you on the face is showing characteristics of the **Fire** element.

- The laid-back golden retriever that loves to take naps and never misses a meal is most likely under the influence of the **Earth** element.

- The Siamese cat whose routine is predictable and likes to be left alone is more than likely displaying qualities of the **Metal** element.

- The orange tabby cat that seemed happiest when caring for her kittens is probably of the **Water** constitution.

- The Rottweiler that chases you out of his backyard will likely be governed by the **Wood** element.

If we clinicians can identify a pet's primary element, then we have a great opportunity to understand his or her predispositions for imbalances and the diseases that they create. We can also use this information to establish dietary, environmental, and behavioral protocols that might help maintain balance and prevent disease.

The Rottweiler that displays characteristics of the Wood element is under the influence of the liver and will be predisposed toward imbalances dealing with internal heat that will often manifest as recurring odorous, moist ear infections and damp skin infections. Animals of a Wood constitution drink lots of water and seek cool places to sleep at night. They also become easily agitated and are prone to developing cancer.

The orange tabby cat with Water-constitution tendencies is dominated by the kidneys and, when imbalanced, tends to develop diseases associated with these organs or the urinary bladder. Many cats with recurring bladder infections have Water constitutions, and knowing these characteristics will help the clinician develop a strategy to help eliminate the root imbalances and prevent persistent problems. Water-element pets often develop arthritis, tend to lose their hearing as they age, and often display fearful behavioral patterns.

The Metal-element pet has defined, sharp angles along the jawline and leg joints. The typical body structure of the Siamese cat is a good example. These pets are dominated by the lungs and are predisposed to upper-respiratory disease and tendencies toward dryness. They are good learners and enjoy routines.

The Earth-constitution pet is the easygoing golden retriever everyone loves. These pets are playful, love attention, and never miss a meal. They are dominated by the spleen, and imbalances often lead to gastrointestinal diseases (usually the pancreas is blamed in Western medicine), fatty tumors, and obesity. They are perpetual worriers and need to get attention, as they do not like to be alone.

Last, but not least, is the Fire-element poodle that is the cheerleader and the life of the party. Fire pets are dominated by the heart and need your approval. They do not like to be controlled by a heavy hand; they need room for exercise; and when imbalanced, they produce excess heat that manifests symptoms such as itching, restlessness, inability to sleep, and manic behavior patterns. These pets like to stay cool at night while sleeping and need foods that will offset their heat production when imbalanced.

Knowing the five elements' characteristics allows clinicians to provide advice to assist the caretaker in establishing balance and preventing disease in their pet.

How Acupuncture Works

Acupuncture is the primary tool for treatment in TCM. According to practitioners, the body is composed of 12 regular meridians that are paired and 2 single meridians, which circulate Qi (energy) and blood throughout the body in order to maintain normal function. There are also 15 collateral meridians, 8 extraordinary channels, and 12 divergent meridians, as well as a number of regional channels that connect the entire body like a system of highways and roads.

The channels and collaterals allow the whole body to communicate and function as an individual unit. However, disease conditions that come from outside the body will often use the same channels and collaterals to penetrate the Zang-Fu organs. We can use meridians to treat both superficial and deep imbalances. Placing acupuncture needles at specific points along these meridians will stimulate the movement of energy and blood and will reestablish normal physiological functions.

Although there is no scientific evidence demonstrating how acupuncture actually works, new technologies involving the body's energy system—such as electrodermal screening, random event generators, quantum scanning, and bioresonance—may help scientists answer this question. The results of performing acupuncture at selected points, however, is documented, consistent, and predictable. There are acupuncture points that control vomiting, stop seizures, eliminate pain, relieve anxiety, reduce stomach acidity, slow or increase bowel motility, stimulate nerve function, and treat shock as well as many other conditions. Using acupuncture is a great alternative to harsh drugs that have potential for harmful side effects.

Acupuncture treatments have a cumulative effect. If the treatments are done once a week consistently, subsequent treatments seem to pick up where the previous treatment left off. With acute or sudden problems, like muscle injuries, acupuncture acts quickly and may take only one treatment to resolve the issue. However, treating chronic conditions, like arthritis and other degenerative diseases, often takes several weeks before improvement becomes obvious, and then will usually require a maintenance schedule, such as monthly treatments. Again, each pet is treated on an individual basis and responds differently.

One concern that caretakers often have when considering acupuncture treatments is whether the needles will cause pain when placed in the skin. Most pets will feel the needles being inserted, but very few resist the treatment due to discomfort. In the many years that I have used acupuncture on hundreds of pets, I've encountered only one that needed to be sedated. I would not have opted to continue the treatment if it weren't for the fact that acupuncture was the only modality I believed would restore function to the dog's paralyzed leg. Most animals, though, are receptive to the process. A cat that I treated for several imbalances allowed me to place 12 acupuncture needles in her face and head without resisting.

For those pets that are nervous and hypersensitive to pain, there are ways to reduce their anxiety, whether it is by placing calming needles in them and then waiting a bit or by offering them treats during the procedure to occupy their attention. I often use frozen peanut butter placed along the rims of plastic cups. Dogs love licking the tasty treat, and one frozen cup will usually divert their attention for about ten minutes.

Many people looking for options for their pets that extend beyond traditional Western medicine will ask questions such as "How many treatments will the pet need?" or "How long will it take before we see the benefits?" These questions are difficult to answer, as many of the problems I see have been going on for extended periods, and trying to get to the root of them and create balance might take some time.

A client of mine who received acupuncture many years ago in San Francisco shared her insight with me from her experience: After receiving treatment for her arthritic neck that caused persistent pain, my client asked the acupuncturist, an elderly Chinese woman, how long it would take before the acupuncture resolved the problem. The woman answered, "How long you take to get there is how long you take to get back."

Chinese Herbal Remedies

Many years ago, after having incorporated the use of acupuncture into my veterinary practice, I was fortunate enough to have a discussion with one of the premier veterinary acupuncturists in the country, Dr. Huisheng Xie. Dr. Xie has been practicing veterinary acupuncture for more than 25 years as well as teaching TCM to veterinarians. His success with directing healing in animals is internationally recognized, yet still he is always ready to help anyone in need of his services.

After one of Dr. Xie's lectures, I asked him specifically what he thought the reason was for his great success in using his modalities to treat animals. His answer was precise: "One-third acupuncture, one-third herbs, one-third God." At that moment, I knew I needed to learn more about Chinese herbal therapy and how it works in conjunction with veterinary acupuncture.

The use of Chinese herbs to treat patients has been documented as far back as the Shang Dynasty (18th–12th centuries B.C.E.). A popular adjunct to acupuncture in both animals and humans, Chinese herbal formulas are used to treat imbalances, ranging from infections, organ failure, and allergies to musculoskeletal diseases, such as arthritis.

To begin understanding how Chinese herbs work, we must take a look at how the herbal formulas are organized. Herbs are categorized initially by their energetic capability to produce a range of temperatures in the body. The five energies are *cold, cool, neutral, warm,* and *hot.* Each temperature designation has physiological characteristics that aid the clinician in determining which herb or herbal formula should be used. For example, cold herbal formulas will act to relieve inflammation, whereas warm herbal formulas stimulate circulation. It's important to remember that Chinese herbal remedies are formulated for body imbalances or patterns, and *not* for specific disease diagnoses.

Chinese herbs are also categorized by their taste—*sour, bitter, sweet, pungent,* and *salty*—each of which promotes a specific TCM function that has a direct effect on the patient's physiology. It is not surprising that there are five categories, as each taste is a quality assigned to one of the five elements:

- Wood (liver) is sour.

- Fire (heart) is bitter.

- Earth (spleen) is sweet.

- Metal (lungs) is pungent.

- Water (kidneys) is salty.

Let's look at an example: Of the Wood element, pineapple is considered sour in taste, acts as an astringent, and helps with digestion. Some clinicians will use pineapple (as well as mango) extracts to supplement deficient digestive enzymes. Digestive enzymes have historically been produced from animal tissue, which is effective but can create a problem if the treated pet has an allergy to that animal (it's more common than you might think). If you use pineapple, however, you avoid the potential side effects.

One of the big advantages of using herbal formulas is that they can easily replace drugs commonly used in veterinary and human treatments. They can also be more cost-effective.

Nutraceuticals

The use of nutraceuticals has exploded in the United States and other countries over the past few years. The term *nutraceutical* is used when a food or food component is taken for its medicinal value, extending beyond its nutritional value. There is evidence that many civilizations throughout history used food medicinally. Hippocrates, considered the father of Western medicine, stated, "Let food be thy medicine." However, the Japanese are credited with starting the current movement in the late 1900s, and today in the United States nutraceuticals have become a billion-dollar industry.

Until several years ago, food in the United States was analyzed based primarily on its nutritional components and categorized as protein, carbohydrate, or fat. Food was also evaluated for its human palatability (taste). There was no investigation of its medicinal value until the nutraceutical industry began to link some foods with specific health benefits. Today, thanks to this movement, we know that carrots contain beta-carotene that benefits the eyes, as well as other parts of the body; antioxidants can be found in grapes, berries, teas, and dark chocolate; cancer-fighting chemicals are present in broccoli; and beneficial omega-3 fatty acids are found in fish.

Research into nutraceuticals works to identify phytochemicals in food that will have a biological effect or health benefit. Thousands of phytochemicals have been identified, and many of them are now being used to treat specific diseases as well as aid the functioning of a healthy body. According to nutraceutical and food-supplement manufacturers that provide products specifically designed for pets, commercial pet foods are altered during processing and lose some of their essential phytochemicals; the supplements are designed to replace those that have been lost. Other formulations provide combinations of food by-products and phytochemicals that are specifically aimed at aiding the body in fighting disease. Examples are Standard Process supplements that support the adrenal glands, kidneys, cardiovascular system, liver, and bowel.

Nutraceuticals, like herbs, are not regulated by the government in the United States, so they have very loose restrictions as to their claims for effectiveness, quality ingredients, and absorbability by the body. These are factors to consider when choosing nutraceuticals for your pet.

Herbal Remedies, Western-Style

Herbal therapy has become popular in the United States as more and more people are looking for natural remedies to replace standard chemical-based pharmaceuticals. Western herbal therapy differs from Traditional Chinese Medicine remedies in that the herbs focus on diseases rather than body imbalances. Although this difference might seem insignificant, it is not. We have to remember that each body, whether human or animal, is a unique system unto itself. To believe that all bodies and diseases will respond identically to an herbal supplement is unrealistic. So, the best we can hope for is enough generalization in therapy (along with our own placebo effect) that we will feel some benefit from taking the herbal supplement.

The Western herbal industry is attempting to extract the medicinal value of certain plants or plant combinations, manufacture a product that can transfer these benefits into the body, and obtain the same effects. This is a very tough goal to achieve. Processing plants without destroying their medicinal value is extremely difficult. The Chinese have spent thousands of years perfecting this process, which is why they have become so proficient at it and why their results are so predictable. But this is not the case with Western herbals available in the United States.

The Food and Drug Administration (FDA) categorizes herbs as dietary supplements, which do not need FDA approval before they are made available commercially. Therefore, scientific investigation into the claims made by the manufacturer are not mandatory. The company simply has to state the benefits on the label and assert that they have research to support their claims. The manufacturer also has to state on the label that their product has not been assessed by the FDA and that it is not to be used for treatment of diseases. Standards for purity are left up to the manufacturer. When a client asks me what herbal supplement or therapy I would recommend for their pet, I always select one manufactured by a company I have confidence in—in other words, their products have delivered beneficial effects that stand the test of time.

Throughout history, most herbal therapy has required the patient to ingest the whole plant or a portion of it, such as the leaf, root, or berry. Nowadays, processing has virtually eliminated this practice, with manufacturers often limiting an herbal remedy to what they believe is the important curative ingredient. Milk thistle, for example, has been used for many years as a natural herbal supplement that may benefit a diseased liver. Research indicates that these benefits probably come from the active ingredient, *silybum marianum,* obtained from the seeds. Currently, there are companies that have extracted and isolated the active ingredient and produce a chemical compound that can be used in veterinary medicine to treat liver disease. These pharmaceutical drugs are sold only by prescription.

When a manufacturer attempts to isolate and retrieve the chemical ingredient that they believe provides a medicinal benefit for a patient, they are forgetting about holism. The benefit of the plant is not limited to the active chemical ingredient. There is so much more! Processing the plant reduces its essence and restricts the benefits derived from the whole. The manufacturer neglects to consider that the plant has an energetic component that is just as beneficial to the patient as a chemical extract. This is why many ancient plant remedies call for consuming the whole plant or administering it in a form that will not reduce it to its parts.

One way to do this is by smoking the plant. When a plant is burned, the patient can breathe in its energetic components. *Artemisia moxa,* a wormwood plant used in Chinese and Japanese medicine, is a good example. Acupuncturists often use moxa treatment to apply heat to specific acupuncture points. The patient benefits from the heat, as well as the energetic components of the plant that directs healing.

It is critical to seek the guidance of a clinician who has knowledge of and experience with herbal remedies if you wish to include them in your pet's health plan. There are too many variables in the herbal industry to wade into this treatment area alone. A lot of people falsely believe that "natural" means healthy and that, because herbs are natural, they don't have potential side effects. On the contrary—many can interfere with other medicines and limit or block their effectiveness. There are also plants that may have natural benefits but can be toxic if taken into the body incorrectly. We must also be aware that a plant is exposed to environmental factors, affecting its essence as well as its potential health benefits. In the past, imported herbs have contained harsh chemicals that are prohibited in the United States. Severe illnesses and deaths have occurred because the herbs were not regulated and inspected.

We also need to be sensitive to the origin of herbs we purchase from other countries. Many plants historically used for medicinal purposes have become so rare that they are now threatened with extinction, and we should be aware that purchasing these plants only further promotes the harvesting of endangered species. Many herb companies will not buy these endangered plants and instead look to obtain the same results with plants that grow in abundance.

Again, we must remember that every individual, as well as every species, will have a specific reaction to an herbal remedy. Some herbs that are readily used for humans can be toxic for a dog or cat. We should also keep in mind that many herbal remedies can alter the effects of pharmaceutical medicines.

However, herbs—when used wisely—can offer tremendous benefits at a low cost and with few side effects.

Aromatherapy and Essential Oils

The use of essential oils derived from plants has been documented for thousands of years. With the inclusion of aromatherapy in an array of holistic modalities, the medicinal use of essential oils has regained some popularity today.

Aromatherapy is based on the principle that certain plants contain essential compounds that have health benefits. As I mentioned previously, the essence (energetic components) of a plant can be transferred through a gaseous compound produced by heating or burning the plant. Essential oils are primarily created by distilling plant oils over heat. This releases the volatile compounds, which are then condensed into an oil-based solution that can be administered to the patient. The oils, which carry the essence of the plant, can be used topically or placed in a nebulizer and heated. The vapor can be inhaled or placed over a flame to produce incense.

Essential oils have been used . . .

- . . . to relieve irritation and inflammation of the skin or mucous membrane.
- . . . to soothe irritation of the lining of the upper-respiratory system.
- . . . to increase resistance to bacteria that might enter through the skin.
- . . . as a diuretic aid.
- . . . to improve disturbed psychological conditions.

There are many grades of essential oils, and their effectiveness is directly related to their quality. Unfortunately, because the FDA categorizes such oils as nutraceuticals, there are no regulatory controls to assure customers of their purity. I recommend that "medical grade" essential oils be used. These oils are routinely more expensive and made by companies whose names are easily recognized.

Some essential oils can be toxic to pets, especially cats. Before using them, consult with your holistic veterinarian for his or her recommendations. Some of the most popular essential oils that may have health benefits include the following:

- **Eucalyptus:** Mostly used for coughs and lung congestion.
- **Lavender:** Very good for skin problems and itching; also good for anxiety.
- **Ginger:** Used routinely for nausea and also effective for motion sickness.
- **Peppermint:** Works as an insect repellent; good for arthritis, sprains, and strains.

Chiropractic Therapy

I include chiropractic care here because this modality is usually considered a complementary form of treatment; it uses neither pharmaceuticals nor surgery. I have personally seen many animals benefit from chiropractic therapy.

Chiropractic therapy, both human and veterinary, has come under great scrutiny in the United States. As with many forms of complementary medicine, the benefits cannot be measured scientifically. As I have discussed previously, without proof the modality will usually be shunned by the medical profession. To make things more confusing, chiropractors in the United States are divided in their opinions of how the modality works.

Chiropractic therapy is based on the form and function of the joints, particularly the spine (vertebral column), which is composed of many bony segments aligned from the top of the head to the tip of the tail. Chiropractors believe that joints can become misaligned, or *subluxated* (partially dislocated), and this subluxation may lead to pain or improper function of the nerves, muscles, and other tissues. By manipulating the affected joint and reestablishing its normal alignment, the chiropractor brings relief from the problem.

As a holistic practitioner, I am aware of the energetic movement throughout the body along fixed pathways, and I am also sure that when any part of the body disrupts this energetic flow, dis-ease occurs. I have had many patients over the years that were slow to respond to acupuncture and herbal remedies; yet after I referred their caretakers to a veterinary chiropractor and the chiropractic work was completed, the pet would return to the clinic and respond remarkably well to the acupuncture and herbs.

Homeopathy

The use of homeopathy in humans and animals began in the early 1800s. A German physician named Samuel Hahnemann believed that a substance causing symptoms similar to those of a specific disease in healthy people could eliminate that disease in sick people. He also believed that the body was composed of an energetic field he termed *the vital force.* In his opinion, physical disease originated as a psychological disturbance that caused a disruption of the vital force. Once damaged, the protective force could be penetrated by disease entities, called *miasms,* creating specific symptoms.

Substances that would produce symptoms similar to those of specific diseases were identified, diluted, and manipulated, so that the final remedy had almost none of the original substance but maintained an ability to mount a defense against the disease. As I have discussed throughout this book, we're learning more every day about subatomic energetic principles, and some homeopaths believe that the energetic component of the remedy acts upon the energetic component of the disease to eliminate it from the body. Today, hundreds of homeopathic remedies are used to treat various conditions.

Like so many complementary forms of treatment, homeopathy has been dismissed by the scientific community as unethical and ineffective. Yet holistic veterinarians throughout the world have been successfully using it to treat animals as an adjunct to pharmaceutical interventions. Homeopathy, like other complementary forms of treatment, focuses on eliminating the root or source of the disease, not just treating symptoms.

Homotoxicology

Homotoxicology is the latest, improved version of homeopathy. It was developed in Germany by Dr. Hans-Heinrich Reckeweg in the early 1900s. This new perspective of promoting healing combined homeopathy with traditional medicine (referred to as allopathic medicine). Reckeweg believed that toxicities, both external and internal, were the source of disease. The deeper the toxicity penetrated the body, the more severe the disease. In his view, the simple, diluted remedies used by traditional homeopaths were ineffective in treating long-standing diseases. He believed that when the vital force (the body's defense system) was deeply penetrated, it would take more than one remedy to restore it back to health. He began to increase the concentration of the active ingredient, as well as combine several remedies. Homotoxicologists describe the process as much like the combining of musical notes (vibrational energy) from individual instruments to create a symphony.

Veterinary homotoxicologists have gravitated to the newer philosophy because it moves away from the homeopaths' belief that psychological and emotional imbalances are at the root of all disease. By focusing on clinical symptoms and physical imbalances, veterinary homotoxicologists can select remedies that appear to be more specific for animals than the traditional individual remedies of homeopathy.

One advantage that homotoxicology appears to have over homeopathy is that this hybrid form of complementary treatment seems to bridge the gap between the conceptual methodologies of most holistic modalities and traditional pharmaceutical-based medicine. The important thing to remember is that homotoxicology is being used today to treat diseases that have either had no effective treatment or required the use of a potentially harmful pharmaceutical compound.

Bach Flower Remedies

Flower remedies are another type of homeopathic treatment. Unlike traditional homeopathic remedies, flower remedies are not subject to dilution modifications and are treated with water exposed to sunlight. Once again, the scientific community contends that there is no evidence that flower remedies are effective. However, I have used Bach Flower Remedies for years and have found them very beneficial for both cats and dogs.

An English scientist named Dr. Edward Bach developed these remedies in the 1930s, and they have been widely used since that time. Bach recognized the benefits some flowers or combinations of flowers had on certain emotional disturbances, which he believed were the primary cause of disease. He claimed that the energetic (essence) of a flower could be extracted by placing the flower in distilled water and passing sunlight through it. He later found that the dilution factor did not matter; it was the energetic component that transferred to the solution. Bach Flower Remedies use many plants for their essential benefits, either alone or mixed with other remedies, to balance emotional disturbances. They are usually given orally to people and pets.

I have found Rescue Remedy—which includes a combination of cherry plum, rock rose, impatiens, clematis, and star of Bethlehem—particularly useful in cats with behavioral imbalances that manifest as fear or aggression. Some concern has arisen about giving Rescue Remedy orally to cats, as the original form contains alcohol. I have not seen any side effects from the alcohol in my patients, but if you're concerned about toxicity, you can steep the liquid remedy before use.

I have also seen this remedy help pets that get extremely nervous when traveling, such as going to the veterinarian or groomer. Two or three drops of Rescue Remedy placed under the tongue about 45 minutes before the trip can relax the pet and make the trip much less stressful.

Ayurvedic Medicine

Ayurvedic medicine, also referred to as *Ayurveda,* is one of the traditional and primary forms of medicine used in India. Ayurveda dates back thousands of years and is a great example of holistic thinking. For an individual (human or pet) to be healthy, there must be balance of body, mind, and spirit. Imbalance in any of these areas results in disease. In the United States, the practice of Ayurveda in humans or animals falls under the category of complementary or alternative modalities (CAM).

The term *Ayurveda* comes from two Sanskrit words, *ayur* and *veda,* and means "the knowledge of life." Practitioners of this ancient form of medicine stress the importance of maintaining physical and emotional balance to prevent disease. Ayurveda practitioners believe that there is interconnectedness among all things in the universe and that maintaining harmony in nature is imperative for personal balance. Disease arises when there is disruption in this harmony.

Ayurvedic medicine is based on the principle that the body is influenced by two factors: the body's *constitution* and its *dosha* (energetic makeup or influences). The body's constitution is the inherent ability for the body to maintain itself as well as protect itself against diseases. The constitution does not change throughout the individual's life, so we will focus on the factor that can be influenced . . .

Doshas

All body functions, mental and physical, are influenced by the doshas. A dosha is the energetic profile of the individual. Unlike in the five elements theory of Traditional Chinese Medicine, the individual has a primary dosha but is also influenced by the other two doshas, much like two smaller circles within a larger circle. The primary dosha is the individual's strength, while the influences of the other doshas can contribute to his or her weaknesses. If the secondary doshas have too much influence, imbalance occurs, which can lead to a range of disease.

The primary and secondary doshas work together in the over-all function of the body. Balance and well-being can be managed through adding to the strength of the primary dosha and reducing input from the minor doshas. Input can be in the form of foods or emotions, for example.

A pet's primary dosha falls into one of three categories: *vata, pitta,* or *kapha.*

— The **vata** dosha is influenced by the wind and is primarily responsible for movement in the mind and body. Anything that flows—energy, blood, lymph, food through the body, and breathing—is controlled by vata. Vata pets are known for their enthusiasm for life and tremendous intelligence, and their frames are usually small and angular. When balanced, these pets have good energy, move quickly, and are independent, as they tend to think for themselves. When imbalanced, they tend to be sensitive to stress in the environment, their coats get dry, and they can become moody. Since vata energy is cool, light, and dry, we try to avoid those influences that are hot, heavy, and oily.

— **Pitta** animals are influenced by fire and water. The primary function of the pitta dosha is transformative, and it's responsible for metabolism and absorption of nutrients. The digestive system, blood, eyes, skin, and tendons are the organs influenced by pitta. Pitta pets are typically medium-build animals, known to enjoy "leading the pack" with their energy and intelligence, and they can be very competitive. They also enjoy eating and drink lots of water. When out of balance, pitta pets can be irritable and even get angry waiting for their food. They tend to produce lots of internal heat, which can lead to skin diseases, eye problems, ear infections, acidic stomachs, and cancer.

— **Kapha** pets are influenced by earth and water, and their energy focuses on overall structure. This dosha is responsible for the body's water functions, such as skin moisture and joint lubrication, as well as the body's stability, including memory capacity and immunity. Its influence can be found at any moist point in the body, such as the chest, sinuses, mucous membranes, and joints. Kapha pets are usually easygoing and relaxed. When in balance, they express themselves with love and affection and are quick to forgive. When out of balance, they can be clingy and greedy. Kapha pets are usually strong, have a heavier build, and are prone to becoming overweight. They can be the pillar of strength at home when others are stressed; however, once they reach their limit, they tend to worry themselves sick. Damp weather is usually bothersome to Kapha pets, and they're prone to developing allergies, congestion, asthma, and fatty lumps.

Deepak Chopra, renowned doctor and Ayurvedic advocate, talks a lot about doshas and explains them using a great analogy. It refers to human behavior, but I think we can make the appropriate comparison to our beloved pets. Chopra says that if you want to see doshas at work, go to the airport. When a flight gets canceled or delayed, you'll notice the passengers start naturally dividing up:

- The **pitta** doshas will start yelling at the flight attendants and airline representatives for the inconvenience they're causing everyone.

- The **vatas** will immediately get on their phones or run to the ticket counter to see if they can book another flight.

- The **kaphas** will be the ones sitting in the airport restaurants, enjoying themselves while they wait for things to be resolved.

Although each individual has a fixed dosha, the energetic profile can be influenced by external and internal forces such as diet, environment, and age. When a practitioner of Ayurvedic medicine identifies a patient's dosha, it allows him or her to not only recognize dosha imbalances that cause disease but also use this information to prescribe a healthy lifestyle—which might include diet change, herbal formulas, balancing teas and aromas, physical exercise, and meditation—to prevent future disease. The practitioner is aware of foods, supplements, and aromas that will naturally balance a particular dosha, as well as those that will aggravate the dosha, create imbalance, and potentiate disease—all through energy exchanges, much like with TCM.

The integration of Ayurveda in veterinary medicine in the United States is new and has great potential. A veterinarian using Ayurveda will employ many of the same protocols noted above to establish dosha profiles in each pet and then determine a holistic plan to prevent imbalances that could lead to disease. Even diets that will benefit a pet's individual dosha are now available.

When searching for complementary forms of healing or treatment for our pets, it's easy to become confused by all the available options. We all want to find the best path to maintaining or restoring well-being.

When I first learned complementary methods to treat my veterinary patients, I, too, was overwhelmed by all the possibilities. Now, after many years of using various forms of alternative modalities for pets, as well as for myself and my family, I am firmly convinced that the type of modality is *not* the important factor. What *is* important is that you believe the one you choose will work. If you have a hard time doing so, then it is not resonating with your energy, and you should avoid it. However, if there is another modality that seems interesting to you, you should certainly look into it.

Try to avoid letting your "reasoning" thinking process get in the way. Instead, get quiet, close your eyes, focus on your breathing, and imagine which form of alternative healing might best suit your pet's situation. In time, the answer might come from your intuitive source, and you may feel yourself drawn to focus on a particular method. Once this happens, you can confidently move into the complementary arena with an open mind and an eager attitude.

CHAPTER TEN

LETTING GO

*"Now he has departed from this strange
world a little ahead of me. That means nothing.
People like us know that the distinction between past,
present, and future is only a stubbornly persistent illusion."*

— ALBERT EINSTEIN

I opened the sliding door and moved into the exam room. Quiet
greeted me. In the center of the room, lying on a worn green quilt,
surrounded by people, was my old friend Bear. Bear wagged his tail
when I approached him and licked my hand as I extended it to pet his
graying head. The golden retriever and I had been friends for many
years, and we had formed a special connection after all the experiences we shared.

Bear was a strapping, energetic five-year-old when I first met him.
He brimmed with the eagerness of life, and it easily spilled over to his
human companion, Hal—a large, older fellow with steel-blue eyes
and a wide smile. The connection between the two was palpable;
each was eager to introduce the other to me.

If it weren't for Bear, Hal would have been mostly alone in the
world. His wife had died several years prior, and his children were
all grown up with busy lives and children of their own. A quiet

knowingness existed between Bear and Hal, a respect for the role each played in the other's life. It was a connection of the heart.

Life moved smoothly for Hal and Bear until the day they entered the exam room for me to check out a lump near Bear's elbow. The bloody, angry mass was aggressive and needed to be removed quickly. The surgery was done that morning. The pathology report that followed cast a dark cloud: The mass had been a malignant cancer that was spreading to other locations in the body and would ultimately lead to Bear's death.

The news hit Hal hard. His blue eyes filled with tears as his four-legged friend rested his head in his lap for support and comfort. I encouraged Hal to try to have faith in the cycle of life and reminded him that it was up to Bear to decide when it was time to go.

Hal agreed that he would try, and then implied that Bear was his whole world. Over the phone Hal's children also expressed concern about what would happen to their father if Bear died. They all agreed that the dog seemed to be the sole reason Hal got up each morning.

I put Bear on a regime of acupuncture and herbal treatments aimed at reestablishing balance in his body. I also recommended supplements and a diet change that would inhibit cancer growth. After the initial phase of treatment, I saw Bear once a month for follow-up treatment and reevaluation. Each month I delivered the good news that there was no sign that the cancer had recurred. Each time the response was the same: a beaming smile from Hal and a wagging tail from Bear as his caretaker gave him a big hug. I am sure the hearts of pet and person were in synchrony.

Then a call came one morning about a year and a half after Bear's initial diagnosis. Hal's daughter wanted to let me know that her father had passed during the night and that his best friend, Bear, was by his side until the end. We shared some tears and a few memories. The children had always wondered who would go first.

Three weeks after Hal was laid to rest, the oldest son brought Bear in for a checkup. Bear was happy to see me, and I couldn't help but feel a sense of contentment and an aura of peace from my old friend. It didn't surprise me to discover that the cancer had returned and had now spread throughout his body. What *did* surprise me was how Bear managed to hold off until Hal passed. The cancer was always meant to return, but only Bear knew when.

Now, in the quiet room, three adult children and six grandchildren surrounded the old dog on the green quilt. They came not only to let him go but to thank him. We all knew that Bear had served his purpose as a loyal companion to Hal, and for this, we all loved him dearly. Suddenly, I could feel Hal's presence in the room, and he steadied my trembling hands as I gave the last injection. Through the tears that flowed freely, I smiled, knowing that the two were together again, with the smile, the hug, and the wagging tail.

Limited Body, Eternal Soul

A holistic approach to pet health necessitates broaching the subject of death. We must expand our ideas about this somber topic in hopes of removing the fears that often accompany it. We have been taught to believe that death is the end of life. What lies beyond it has always been a deep mystery.

To understand death, we must first look at its opposite, life itself. In his book *Getting in the Gap,* popular spiritual teacher and author Dr. Wayne Dyer described life as "coming from no-where into now-here and then returning to no-where." This metaphorical description is a great way to appreciate that although what we call "life" and "death" appear dramatically different, in actuality they are simply two aspects of the never-changing, eternal journey of the soul. It is just a matter of shifting our perspective.

We often think of death as the time when the body dies—whether due to illness, trauma, or old age. The truth is that our physical bodies are in a continual process of death and rebirth as cells die and are replaced by new ones. You literally have an entirely different body, with none of the same cells, every few years. If you think of yourself (or your pet) as only "the body," you could say that you have actually died countless times throughout your life. You just don't realize that it is happening.

Every cell, tissue, and organ dies and is replaced so that you can continue inhabiting a functioning body here on Earth. Surely you can see that *you* are not your cells, nor are you the parts of the body that the cells make up, like a leg or a liver. And finally, you are not the whole body, either. Though you may identify with your body, it is merely the vehicle in which you pass through life. Your true, inner self is the only part of you that doesn't change.

In our pets, just as in each and every one of us, there is an eternal self that existed before this body and will continue to exist after this body has died. This eternal self has been called by many names: the soul, the spirit . . . The name is not important, but for our purposes, let's call it the soul. What matters is the realization that your pet's true identity is not the body, but the eternal soul. (A wise young guru was once asked, "Do animals have souls?" He answered, "Of course they do. All you have to do to realize this is to look into their eyes.")

The body has a tremendously important function. Without it, we could not experience life as we do. We could not use our physical senses to enjoy our surroundings, have relationships with others, or co-create our lives as organic beings. However, we are not our bodies. As many spiritual thinkers and luminaries throughout history have said in a variety of ways, we are souls living in bodies to have an earthly experience.

If we can entertain the idea that when our pets' bodies die, their true selves (the soul) live on, then we can eliminate some of the pain associated with the finality of death, the pain of separation. We can understand that our souls are still connected and always will be throughout time. As I have emphasized throughout this book, there is a oneness that connects all things. (Hindus, for example, call this connection the *Atman.*) Therefore, we can never be separated from our loved ones, not in life and not in death.

A child's first exposure to death usually involves a pet or grandparent. At some level of consciousness, we accept the fact that we will probably outlive our pets, but when the time comes to say good-bye to our beloved friends, nothing can eliminate the pain of letting go.

In what seems like the blink of an eye, the bouncing puppy transformed into a wise, old dog. Gray whiskers surround his warm brown eyes. Just yesterday he roamed the outdoors, always looking back to find you, ready to swim the lake or fetch the stick, always willing to please. Today, things have changed. He still wags his tail, but his legs no longer support him. He wants to run through the hills again, but his body tells him that it is time to go. He wants to be there for you, and he feels you grieving. But you love him too much to allow him to continue to be in this diminishing condition, and you know that you must do what is right.

Whether to Intervene

When it becomes clear that a beloved pet's quality of life is diminishing, either through illness or simply old age, some people choose not to intervene and prefer to let their animal companion die naturally. This is perfectly acceptable if we can eliminate any symptoms that cause discomfort. For a pet to die at home is the most natural situation I can imagine. But I would recommend that you allow the pet time alone. The time for transition is up to the pet, and sometimes it can be difficult for him or her to let go if you are there. The pet feels your anxiety and grief and wants to comfort you by not moving on. You must always keep the best interest of the pet foremost in your mind, telling him or her that it is all right to go and that you are thankful for his or her loving friendship.

When I talk to people about a pet's right to determine his or her own time to go, I always think of Dusty, a lovely cocker spaniel that showered love on her family for 12 years. In the end, Dusty's kidneys failed incurably, and her human companions did not want to have her put to sleep. So Dusty was treated with intravenous (IV) fluids around the clock with her companions by her side. Each morning she would come to the clinic for evaluation and treatment, and her two caretakers would sit next to her cage throughout the day. Then, when the clinic closed, Dusty was taken home and monitored by her companions until the clinic opened the following morning.

One morning as Dusty was placed in her cage, it was obvious that her IV catheter had obstructed and needed to be replaced. The dog seemed to be feeling fine, and her human companions decided that, while we were replacing the catheter, they would go down the street and have a cup of coffee. The car had just left the parking lot when Dusty rolled on her side and died. It was the first time that she had been away from her human friends, and it had offered her the opportunity to transition.

When a pet's quality of life has diminished and can no longer improve, it is time to make the decision to let the pet go. This is a blessing for the pet as well as the caretaker. We often forget that when our pet is ill or in pain, we also have a tendency to suffer. I have seen emotional suffering in families with dying pets that is just as palpable as the pet's condition.

When pain is not a factor, the decision is based on how we define *quality of life.* Unfortunately, there is a vast difference of opinion, and this is where problems can arise. If the time comes when a caretaker must admit that the quality of life is gone and intervention will not improve the situation, he or she alone can make the decision to help the pet transition. But when a couple or family is involved, it becomes a bit more complicated. Often I see families arguing over whether it is the right time to put the pet to sleep. This can lead to additional suffering when emotions are already intense. In these situations, it is best to respect the feelings of others. Let the decision be made with calm hearts and minds.

Many times over the years I have watched one spouse talk the other into making the decision when he or she was not ready. This undoubtedly led to resentment and produced an emotional scar that was slow to heal. My advice is to be patient and understanding and respect the fact that your partner might not be emotionally prepared to let go. Trying to force the decision with opinions and facts leads only to distress and negative energy in an environment that is already tense. Given time and space, without pressure, most of us can see clearly what is needed.

Carolyn was one such client who could come to a decision once she gave herself the quiet space to receive it. Carolyn came to me when a golf ball–size tumor was found in her cat Rosa's heart muscle. She was shocked and shattered, and looking to me for a solution.

You see, Carolyn had come to my office out of desperation. Rosa was just a few days over 12 years of age and had a good, healthy life. Carolyn was caught off guard by the possibility that, in a very short while, she would be facing life without her beloved cat. Her veterinarian sent her to a specialist as soon as the cancer was detected because it was a type that is beyond the scope of most general practitioners.

The specialist, with her tools and knowledge, could provide little hope for Rosa, but she did offer chemotherapy. Carolyn couldn't imagine doing something that seemed so brutal to Rosa to extend her life by only a few more weeks. The quart of clear fluid that the specialist drained from Rosa's chest did help her breathe easier, but Carolyn and the specialist knew that in a few days the fluid would return.

"The specialist said that the chemotherapy might buy her some time. I know that it would be tough for her. You know, the side effects and all. I don't want her to suffer, but I don't want to give up too soon!" she cried.

Taking a step back from the pull of emotions, it was clear what was happening. Life had presented Carolyn with a problem that could not be solved. No matter how much she considered all her apparent options, she could not sort through the information and marshal enough evidence to make a sound decision one way or the other. The more she thought about what she needed to do, the more she suffered, and the suffering led her further and further away from the answer she so desperately needed.

Carolyn came to me hoping I could provide some alternative method for treating her cat's tumor, one that wasn't so harsh. Maybe that would give her another option she could weigh and help her with the decision that was consuming her life.

Even though I didn't know Carolyn, I knew enough about the truth of the matter that I believed my recommendations would fall on keen ears. I asked her if she could find a way to stop struggling for the answer. Then I explained to her that the answer was already there; she just had to move out of the way and let it reveal itself. Like seeking an object that has fallen into a pool of water, we can gain clarity only when we stop desperately splashing and allow the surface to be still and reveal what we are looking for.

I told Carolyn that when we *react* to fearful situations, which most of us have been conditioned to do, we often interfere with the guidance that is always within us. If we can trust our inner truth to find us, it will usually take us in the direction we need to go. These ideas weren't foreign to Carolyn, but I was reminding her of a deeper truth within her that she had temporarily forgotten. She agreed that she could let her reactive mind take a backseat.

Two days had passed when I received a note from Carolyn: "I found the quietness that I needed, and I realized that I had lost sight of my compassion. When I regained that state of mind, the direction came, and I let her go with no regrets, no doubts."

When we are faced with decisions, we have two ways that we can seek the answer: We can use our rational minds, and hopefully our experience and knowledge will give us enough data to allow us to make a choice. Or we can move beyond the rational mind and open our awareness to the larger truth, and our intuition will guide us comfortably along our pathway.

You should be aware that your choices aren't limited to medical intervention or putting an animal to sleep. Should you come to the understanding that it is time to let go, you can receive help in making your companion as comfortable as possible until the pet decides he or she is ready. Animal hospice is becoming very popular and offers a great opportunity for care for both pets and their people during the letting-go process. Many veterinary hospitals are offering hospice services, as are organizations such as the International Association of Animal Hospice and Palliative Care (iaahpc.org). Hospice services aid with treatments, planning, and grieving at a time when most people are having trouble making decisions, due to intense emotions.

When to Let Go

The most difficult question I am asked by my clients is "How do I know when it is time to let go?" When I was a young clinician, it was easy for me to focus on the obvious symptoms: pain, loss of appetite, inability to get up, lack of control over bodily functions, and so on. If there was enough evidence to support the decision, then it must be correct. This approach seemed to help, but it was lacking something vital. Now, as I am older and a bit more seasoned, I understand that these decisions are not supposed to be made by the rational mind. Sure, rational processes give us evidence, but the ultimate decision comes directly from the heart.

I have found that if you take some uninterrupted time with your pet and let your mind go still, you have the ability to connect at a much deeper level of consciousness. It is at this level of connection that you will know your pet's situation and become empathetic with it. Once this level of awareness is attained, you will likely become attuned to whether the time is right. As we've discussed before, intuitive thoughts can come in a variety of forms—you may have a physical sensation, see an image in your mind, or even have a thought or voice pop into your awareness. It may take several occasions with your pet before you experience this connection, but if you are determined and you quiet your mind, the answers will come.

Sometimes we need to be reminded that death is part of the larger circle of life and that even though the body is gone, the essence of our pets will be with us forever. I like to think of Annie, my golden retriever, who would walk with me down the lane by the river. It has been several years since Annie died, but she still accompanies me on my walks. I can picture her bouncing through the brush and lying in the shallow water of the river. My heart still swells, and I know that she is with me.

During this highly emotional time, there is often much confusion and indecision. The first thing to remember when you are considering putting your pet to sleep is that there is no right or wrong. Everyone has an opinion, but it is only your pet and you who will know when it is time. Your veterinarian will probably give you sound advice that will help in making the decision. Then, of course, sometimes the decision seems too difficult to make, and a gentle nudge from the veterinarian can be a blessing.

Children Saying Good-bye

To me, nothing tugs at the heartstrings more than watching a child say good-bye to his or her pet. Often the child is confused and cannot understand all that is happening. I recommend preparing children for the imminent death but keeping them away from the decision process. Allow them to make their own choice as to whether they want to be with the pet during the procedure. Support their emotional needs and let them know that grieving is part of the letting-go process; it is natural and nothing to be ashamed of. Then, when the time comes, the children can be part of the decision to get a new pet and will continue to have fond memories of the animal that is no longer with them.

I am reminded of a couple who came to me in deep despair over how their young son would react to letting go of the family dog. The dog was old and arthritic, and his quality of life was very poor. Their concern for the boy's emotional welfare during the procedure was touching.

When the time came, the boy sat in the chair patiently while the parents gave loving support to the dog. When it was over, the parents turned to comfort the child. The mother asked the boy, "Honey, are you all right?"

The boy looked into his mother's eyes and answered, "Yes. Now can we get a monkey?"

Children are truly amazing and resilient, but we must work to facilitate their emotional growth. In this case, the child's response made it clear that, because his parents had prepared him for what was to happen, he was at ease with the decision.

Other Family Pets

I also believe that it is appropriate to let other pets in the family spend some time with the dying pet before he or she transitions, if possible. While no one knows what goes on in the surviving pets' minds, I hope that, in some way, connecting with the dying pet will help their grieving process.

Pets' responses to the loss of one of their animal friends are all different. It's best to assume that they will suffer some grief, too, and act accordingly. A survey conducted in 1995 by the American Society for the Prevention of Cruelty to Animals found that 50 percent of dogs and cats had reduced appetites after the loss of an animal friend, and 35 percent slept more during the grieving period.

I am reminded of a client couple who had three lovely Chinese shar-peis. Two of the dogs were around 12 years of age, and the other was about 4. When 12-year-old Tango died of a complicated heart condition, his companion Cash took it very hard. She moped around, refused food, and seemed to give up. Her human companions spent extra time with her, doing the things they thought she would enjoy. But it wasn't enough, and within a month she became ill and died from kidney failure. The loss of two of their dogs within such a short period was devastating to the couple. And they were concerned about the emotional state of the remaining younger dog, Lola.

Lola seemed to take the loss of her two companions better than expected, and before long, she was back to her old self. The couple began to wonder if Lola needed a companion, as she was left alone when they were at work. They consulted an animal communicator, who had a long discussion with Lola. It seemed that Lola was enjoying the individual attention from both of her human friends, and she was in no hurry to welcome another dog into the house.

Another one of my clients lived with two cats: Bitsy and Boo. Bitsy was a handful. She ruled the roost and was known to get a bit aggressive with newcomers in the house. On more than one occasion, Bitsy would come up to a visitor, and when the person reached to pet her, she'd take a nip at the stranger and run off with a "Now you know who's boss!" attitude. Boo, on the other hand, was the ultimate lap cat. She loved to spend time receiving affection, whether it came from the people she lived with or a visitor.

Bitsy transitioned first, and Boo was left as the only pet in the household. To everyone's surprise, it seemed that Boo took on Bitsy's personality! She became more aggressive with visitors, like Bitsy, and would often bite her caretakers' hands.

Both stories serve to show that we never know what goes on in the mind of a pet that loses an animal companion. If we're open to it, working with an animal communicator can be especially beneficial to relieve the anxiety and stressful emotions the pet may feel after the loss of a companion. Remember that animal communicators are gifted at quieting their left-hemisphere, busy, thinking mind and receiving guidance through their right-hemisphere, intuitive mind. They can connect to the source energy by raising their awareness or consciousness to a higher dimension where there is no physical boundary between themselves and the pet, and thus they're able to intuit what the pet is feeling. If we can figure out what's causing a pet's emotional upset, we can offer support and healing. Additionally, animal communicators can help us understand what the pet wants or needs from us as part of that support.

Practical Considerations

Once you elect to help your pet transition, you will have to decide whether you want to be present. Most people want to be with their pet to give love and support, but some don't feel that they have the emotional strength to watch. Again, there is no right or wrong. Do what your heart tells you. Your pet never doubted your love and will not start now.

I remember a time when a family had made the decision to let their old dog go. The husband was to be with the dog while the wife was supporting their young daughter in the waiting room. As I prepared to give the injection, I turned and looked at the husband. He was desperately grieving, and I knew in an instant that he did not want to witness this sad event and that he was doing so out of a sense of obligation. I smiled at him and told him that it was all right if he chose not to be in the room. He started crying and thanked me as he gave a last pat to his dog, and then left.

It's important to care for yourself as much as you do the other loved ones in your life. Allow yourself to ask your veterinarian any questions that you may have, and allow your children to ask you any questions that come up for them. If we feel that someone we view as honest and caring has informed us of everything that will happen and has eased our fears, we are able to move forward more easily.

If possible, I recommend that you have your veterinarian come to the house to do the procedure. You want this to be as comfortable as possible for your pet, and being hauled to the veterinary clinic is typically not what the pet would prefer. Not all veterinarians offer this service, but usually there is one nearby who understands the value of a house call.

Another option to consider is a veterinary acupuncturist, if you have access to one. Most are aware of an acupuncture-point combination that will allow a burst of energy to flood throughout the pet's body. This is a temporary treatment that lasts about 24 hours, but allows the pet to improve dramatically the day before the euthanasia is performed. This may give you and your pet one more quality day to spend together.

Another element of your pet's end-of-life process to think about is what to do with the body after euthanasia. I highly recommend that you address this concern in advance and make any necessary arrangements. Most people choose to bury a pet, and I smile fondly when I think of my old cat, Orange Boy, buried on a hilltop overlooking a beautiful Montana mountain range. I could only hope to be so lucky when my time comes.

There is something special about a family sharing their last loving words over a recently buried pet. Unfortunately, in some cities it is illegal to bury a pet in the yard, and other arrangements have to be made. Often there are pet cemeteries that offer burials, and some people enjoy being able to go visit the grave.

Others might choose to have their pet cremated, either keeping the ashes or scattering them in some special place. One of my clients had his beloved dog cremated, and the ashes were dispersed over a favorite river where he and his four-legged friend spent many days hunting together.

Many caretakers are deeply concerned about the handling of their pets' remains—clients often ask me if the cremation facility would deceptively mix their pet's ashes with another pet's. Over the years, I have found the people who offer cremation services to be caring, compassionate individuals, who are aware of the emotions involved with losing a pet. Again, don't be afraid to ask questions. Many facilities do individual cremations so that you can be assured that the remains you receive are only those of your pet.

Grieving and Gratitude

Letting an aging or sick pet go is a trying and emotional event in our lives, but grieving is a natural part of the process, and resisting it can be very detrimental. Don't be surprised if you think you're finished grieving, and suddenly you're gripped with an unexpected pang of sorrow and flow of tears. Grieving has a life of its own, and it's important to honor the process.

Remembering those loving times spent together can often ease the pain. My wife focuses on the sense of gratitude she feels for having shared so much love and life with each pet she has lost, and she often can't tell if she's crying tears of joy or sorrow. The line between grief and gratitude can be very fine. Grieving is intricately intertwined with love and compassion, and it is to be honored, not shamed. I've heard it said that with each loss, our hearts grow. I want to believe that with each loss, we *know* our hearts even more.

Over the years, I've frequently been asked how long the human companion should wait before replacing their deceased pet. This is a difficult question to answer, as each person has his or her own appropriate grieving period. Too often, I have seen grieving people immediately run out and obtain a new pet, hoping to reduce their pain. I have also seen caretakers try to replace the lost pet with another of similar appearance. One client immediately purchased a new poodle with the same physical appearance of the one she had lost. She even went so far as to give it the same name. It was no surprise that she had difficulty establishing a bond with the new pet. Her need to replace the old pet put too much pressure on the new relationship, and both parties suffered.

Grieving is part of the letting-go process, and it must run its course before a decision is made about getting another pet. No pet can ever be replaced. Each has a unique personality that is a God-given, irreplaceable gift. The best we can hope for is to fill that void in our lives with love for a new pet. We must accept that, with time, space will be cleared to introduce another into our hearts, and the new pet will establish his or her own valuable relationships with human and animal companions. Time is a great ally.

AFTERWORD

We have come to the end of our journey together, but *your* journey through holistic pet care is just beginning! The holistic approach to life encompasses caring for and making choices for our pets but also extends to a greater understanding of our interconnectedness. And here we find clarity and understanding that can come only with the experience of sharing our lives with a loving animal companion.

It is important that you remember that your pet entered your life to help you have a better awareness of who you really are. Each experience that comes from that relationship is a blessing.

When pets face illness and disease, the conditioned response is an attempt to regain control and return things to normal. But these are the times when you need to step back, let the fearful thoughts and emotions pass, and allow the experience to reveal itself in its wholeness. The hidden message is a lesson in love.

Having witnessed the pet-caretaker bond over the many years in my veterinary practice, I understand that the energetic relationship between people and their beloved animals is not unlike the one that exists between parent and child. Words such as *natural* and *unconditional* are often used to describe both relationships. These relationships offer an opportunity to experience genuine connection; most humans relate to their pets without the fearful defenses created by the ego. When we remove the ego from the situation, we can feel the energetic bond and experience the unity that occurs with it. There is no longer an apparent separation between entities, and, if needed, healing can be directed.

There is an awareness in all of us—if we take the time to connect to it—that reveals the truth that our pets are our projections of ourselves: who we really are, and who we aspire to be. All things we see in our beloved pets are within us; in our relationship with them, they become like a reflection in the mirror. Our pets reveal to us that we are loving, kind, and compassionate beings living joyfully.

When we adopt the holistic perspective toward our pets and our relationship with them, we see the benefits of maintaining this perspective with *all* of our life experiences. In time, we might see our frailties, our imperfections, and our limitations reflected back to us. But we will also find that potential to love unconditionally, live in the present moment, and savor the simple pleasures of life. I wish that joy for you and your pet, now and forever.

— Dr. Dennis Thomas

SUGGESTED READING

*The Biology of Belief: Unleashing the Power of Consciousness, Matter &
Miracles,* by Bruce Lipton, Ph.D.

*The Extraordinary Healing Power of Ordinary Things: Fourteen Natural
Steps to Health and Happiness,* by Larry Dossey, M.D.

The Field: The Quest for the Secret Force of the Universe, by Lynne
McTaggart

Guardians of Being: Spiritual Teachings from Our Dogs and Cats, by
Eckhart Tolle

You Are the Placebo: Making Your Mind Matter, by Dr. Joe Dispenza

ACKNOWLEDGMENTS

This book would never have been completed without the care and devotion of my wife, Lesa. She has been a motivator, a partner, an editor, a contributor, and a source of unending guidance throughout the process. She has been a mentor in matters of the spiritual pathway, and her devotion to our pets has been a continual source of inspiration. I will always be grateful.

I would also like to extend my gratitude to Ally Machate for her superb editing, and all the folks at Hay House who have helped me bring this book to life.

ABOUT THE AUTHOR

Bethany Anne Taylor Photography

Dr Dennis W. Thomas has been a practising veterinarian for more than 30 years. Throughout most of his career, he focused on a traditional approach to medicine and surgery. After 20 years, he expanded his field of practice to include a more holistic approach.

Trained in Traditional Chinese Medicine at Colorado State University, Dr Thomas became a certified veterinary acupuncturist and then further expanded his practice to include Chinese and Western herbal therapy. He also became interested in energy medicine and learned Reiki, the Japanese method of using the hands to move energy. Having had great success with guided meditation and healing by intention, he recently released a guided-meditation CD as an aid in healing pets.

As a member of the American Holistic Veterinary Medical Association, Dr Thomas gives lectures about holistic pet health and complementary modalities. He has written numerous articles on the benefits of alternative approaches in pet health care. His practice now focuses on promoting healing instead of fighting disease. Dr Thomas works with pets and their people at his Little Healing Room in Spokane, Washington.

www.drdennisthomas.com

Lightning Source UK Ltd.
Milton Keynes UK
UKOW06f1336180815

257105UK00008B/170/P